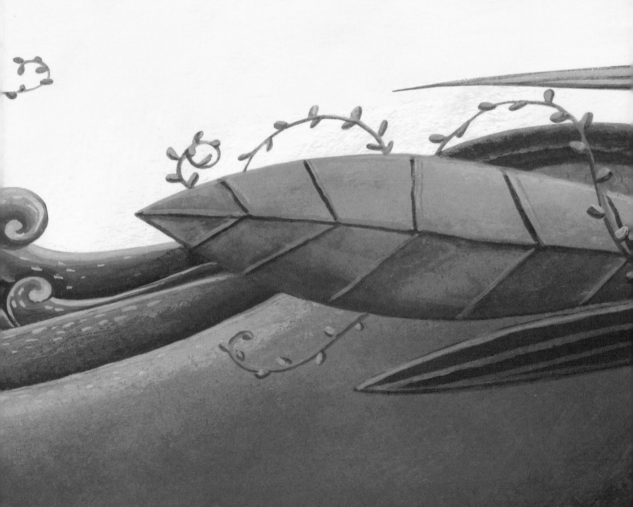

Jesus Calling®

BIBLE STORYBOOK

For:

_____

From:

_____

Date:

_____

Jesus Calling®
BIBLE STORYBOOK

DEDICATION

To the parents and grandparents
who invest time and energy in reading this
Bible storybook to their children and grandchildren.

Your loving involvement in reading these stories
and answering questions is commendable—
and absolutely essential!

Also, to Elie, John, and all the little children
who grow closer to Jesus through the words
and illustrations on these pages.

Jesus said, *"Let the little children come to me . . .*
for the kingdom of heaven belongs to such as these."
Matthew 19:14

Jesus Calling®

BIBLE STORYBOOK

By *Sarah Young*

WITH JEAN FISCHER

Illustrated by CAROLINA FARÍAS

Tommy NELSON®

A Division of Thomas Nelson Publishers

NASHVILLE DALLAS MEXICO CITY RIO DE JANEIRO

Jesus Calling® Bible Storybook
© 2012 Sarah Young

Published in Nashville, Tennessee, by Tommy Nelson. Tommy Nelson is a registered trademark of Thomas Nelson, Inc.

Tommy Nelson titles may be purchased in bulk for educational, business, fund-raising, or sales promotional use. For information, please e-mail SpecialMarkets@ThomasNelson.com.

Design by Koechel Peterson & Associates, Inc., Minneapolis, MN

Library of Congress Cataloging-in-Publication Data:

Young, Sarah, 1946-
    Jesus calling Bible storybook / Sarah Young ; illustrated by Carolina Farías.
       p. cm.
    ISBN 978-1-4003-2033-2 (hardcover)
  1. Bible stories, English. 2. Bible--Devotional use--Juvenile literature. I. Farías, Carolina. II. Title.
    BS551.3.Y68 2012
    220.9'505--dc23

                   2012007532

Printed in China

13 14 15 16 17 RRD 9 8 7 6 5

Special thanks go to:

MacKenzie Howard, the project manager who worked so tirelessly and effectively on this book—wearing many hats, as needed. I always appreciate my publisher, Laura Minchew, who shepherds my publishing and finds wonderful ways to bring the message of Jesus Calling® to children.

I also want to thank Kris Bearss, my editor and friend who works with me on everything I publish.

I'm grateful that Jean Fischer, who compiled the Bible stories, and Carolina Farías, the storybook illustrator, lent their considerable talents to this project.

Finally, I thank my husband, Stephen Young, for providing clear biblical oversight—helping us keep the stories true to God's perfect Word.

Dear Parents and Grandparents,

Nothing warms my heart more than a little blond girl with big blue eyes and an irresistible smile: my granddaughter, Elie Marie. As we welcome her baby brother, John Elliot, into our family, I realize how supremely important it is to help these precious children—and all children— develop a personal relationship with Jesus.

The *Jesus Calling® Bible Storybook* is designed to help young children come to know God's Word and enjoy the Presence of Jesus in their lives. This book tells the wonderful story of God's great love for His people. It shows that the center, the beginning, and the end of this story all focus on Jesus. Not only is Jesus central in the Bible, but He is also central in our lives. Just as He was there when Adam and Eve had to leave the Garden, when Noah built the ark, and when Moses encountered God in the burning bush, Jesus is with us every moment of every day. Because of His sacrifice on the cross, forgiveness and eternal life are promised to all of us who call on His Name— trusting Him as Savior.

As you may know, the devotional *Jesus Calling* was created after years of personal study, prayer time, and journaling. I had kept prayer journals for years, but I yearned for more and more of God in my life. So I set aside time to listen in His Presence and write down what I believed He was saying to me. Thus, my journaling changed from monologue to dialogue. This new way of communicating with God became the high point of my day. I knew these writings were not inspired as Scripture is, but they helped me grow much closer to God. In fact, listening to Jesus increased my intimacy with Him more than any other spiritual discipline. So I shared some of my writings in *Jesus Calling*—to help others who are searching for a deeper experience of Jesus' Presence and Peace. The Bible is, of course, the only Word of God, and I always endeavor to write in accordance with that unchanging standard.

It is my hope that the children who enjoy this Bible storybook will know early in life that they can call on Jesus and He will answer. I pray that they will listen as He speaks to them through His Word and that they will understand how very much He loves them. It's natural for children to love those who love them, so this is the ideal way for them to develop love for Jesus at a young age.

With the Bible stories, I have included *Jesus Calling* devotions in the same style as the adult devotional but at a level that is easy for young ones to understand. They will learn about David and Goliath, Daniel and the lions, and so many other stories. They will also learn about glorifying God and living in ways that please Him.

May you and your loved ones delight in Jesus' Presence and grow in His grace as we joyfully await His return.

Bountiful Blessings!
Sarah Young

THE NEW TESTAMENT

THE OLD TESTAMENT

God's Big Plan | from Genesis 1

A, B, C . . . 1, 2, 3 . . . Everything begins somewhere. Imagine a place with nothing to see, hear, taste, touch, or smell. No earth. No sky. In the beginning, there was nothing but God the Father, His Son—Jesus—and the Holy Spirit.

God had a plan to create something big.

On the first day, God said, "Let there be light," and light happened! God called it *daytime*. The darkness He called *night*. On the second day, God separated the sky and the waters, and on the third, He created land. Water whirled and swirled all around. God gathered the waters into seas, and then up came land: hills, mountains, valleys, and plains.

God spoke again, and plants sprouted from the earth. Colorful flowers of every kind. Vegetables. Trees tall and strong, their branches loaded with plump, juicy fruit. God saw it all, and He said, "This is good!"

On the fourth day, God created the sun and popped the moon in the sky. God hung more stars than you could ever count!

But He wasn't finished yet.

God created birds and sea creatures on the fifth day. Little minnows and giant whales. Tiny hummingbirds and tall ostriches!

Day six was really special! God filled the earth with animals. Worms wiggled in the dirt. Giraffes reached for the sky. Lions roared. Monkeys laughed.

Animals, animals everywhere!

But He still wasn't done.
What do you think God made next?

Jesus Calling

*"I am the Alpha and the Omega,
the Beginning and the End, the First and the Last."*

REVELATION 22:13 NKJV

I am the Alpha and the Omega. That means the
Beginning and the End. Most people call Me Jesus.
I am God the Son. I made the heavens and the earth.
Even then—long before you were born—
I thought of you and I loved you.

God Starts a Family

from Genesis 1

God said, "Let Us make man in Our image, in Our likeness, and they can rule over what We have created."

22

God saved His best for last. He made a man and then a woman, breathing life into them so they had bodies and spirits. God loved them more than anything else. They were the start of His big family.

God made a wonderful Garden for them to live in. Adam and Eve were happy in their perfect new home. They had everything they needed and plenty of delicious food to eat. They could eat the fruit from every tree in the Garden except for one . . .

Adam and Eve's Big Mistake | from Genesis 3

God said, "Don't eat the fruit from the Tree of the Knowledge of Good and Evil. If you eat the fruit, you will die."

God has a terrible enemy named Satan. Satan is evil, and he always wants people to do bad things. He came into that beautiful Garden pretending to be a snake. He slithered around that one tree and whispered to Eve, "You won't die. If you eat this fruit, you will learn about good and evil, and you will be like God."

Satan lied.

But the woman chose
to believe him instead of God.

She ate the fruit. Adam did too.
All at once, God's perfect world changed.
When the man and woman broke God's rule,
something called *sin* entered the world.

And that made God sad.

God made clothes to cover them because they were ashamed. Adam and Eve could no longer live in His perfect Garden of Eden. God had to send them away, where work would be hard and life would be painful.

But God had a plan. He would come to earth as a baby and grow to be a man who would defeat Satan and rescue God's children. Jesus would be His name.

Jesus Calling

No power in the sky above or in the earth below—
indeed, nothing in all creation will . . .
separate us from the love of God.

ROMANS 8:39 NLT

I was there when Adam and Eve left the Garden forever. Wherever they went, I was with them—watching over them. Do you know that I am with you too? Nothing can separate you from My Love.

Cain and Abel, Two Brothers

from Genesis 4

Adam and Eve had two sons. Cain was a farmer, and Abel was a shepherd. They each decided to give God a gift. Cain gave God some of his crops, but Abel sacrificed his best lamb—something he really wanted to keep.

Although Cain and Abel both gave gifts to God, Abel trusted God and gave his best to Him. And so God accepted Abel's gift, but He was unhappy with Cain's. He scolded Cain. That made Cain mad, even jealous of his brother.

Later, the two brothers were in a field, and Cain felt so angry that he killed Abel! He wasn't sorry either. But God saw what happened. "Cain, where is your brother?" He asked.

"I don't know," Cain lied. Cain was punished by God for his great sin, and for the rest of his life he was a wanderer who never got to stay in one place for very long.

Jesus Calling

"If you do good, I will accept you. . . .
Sin wants you. But you must rule over it."

GENESIS 4:7 ICB

When you are angry or you're about to do something bad, come to Me and I will help you. I want you to do what is right and trust Me, as Abel did. I like that kind of faith. I am always near you—ready to help.

The Story of Noah | from Genesis 6–9

Adam and Eve had Cain. Cain had children . . . his children had children . . . and their children had children. The earth became full of people. Sadly, most of them forgot about God and did bad things. This filled His heart with pain.

God was so sad about it that He had to stop it. He wanted to make the world better.

There was one man in all the world who walked with God. His name was Noah.

God told him, "Noah, build an ark and pack it with enough food for you and your family and for the male and female animals I will send your way. Then enter the boat—all of you."

Noah did what God said. And the animals came in pairs—lions and lambs, butterflies and horses, bluebirds and bears, foxes and elephants.

Just as God had told Noah, it began to rain. First just a little. Then big raindrops pounded the earth. Hundreds of raindrops. Thousands. Millions. Billions. Trillions! There was so much water that the ground started to flood. And Noah's ark, which carried Noah, his family, and every kind of animal in the world, started to float.

Before long, the whole earth was covered with water. God's flood destroyed the bad things and washed them all away. Yet everyone and everything in the ark were safe and sound because Noah did what God said.

After forty days and forty nights, the rain stopped.
The sun came out. Slowly the water went down.
God's boat came to rest on top of a tall mountain.

Noah sent out a dove
to look around. It had no
place to land, so it came back
to the ark.

Noah waited seven days and then sent it out again; it returned with a fresh olive leaf in its beak. "The flood is over!" Noah shouted. "Trees are growing again!"

To celebrate the world's new beginning, God hung a rainbow in the sky. "I will never again use a flood to destroy the earth," God said. "This rainbow is My promise to all of My people."

God knew that bad things would happen again. But He already had another plan. One day, He would send His Son, Jesus, to save His children from evil.

Jesus Calling

[The Lord] will cover you with his feathers.
He will shelter you with his wings. His faithful promises
are your armor and protection.
PSALM 91:4 NLT

Trust Me, My child, and don't be afraid. I take care of My children. Just as a mother bird covers her babies with her wings to protect them, I cover you with promises of My Love. When you see a rainbow in the sky, remember My loving care of Noah's family. Then think about how much I love *you*!

The Tower to the Heavens | from Genesis 11

God made people so they could jump and run and do all sorts of wonderful things. God also created us to work together to do great things for Him. Everyone should thank God for these gifts, but sometimes people try to use their skills for themselves instead. That's what happened at a place called Babel.

Rather than saying that God was great and thanking Him, the people began to fill up with pride, thinking that *they* were great. In fact, they thought they were as great as God.

"Let's build a tower to the heavens," they said. "One that will be remembered forever. We can stand on top. People will look up and say, 'Wow! They're something special.'"

God didn't want the people to become so full of pride. If He didn't stop them, they would become as sinful as people were before the big flood. And God cared about them too much to allow that to happen.

To stop them, God confused their speech.

"Camel your bucket hat, no?" said one.
"Hairy bird's feet up top!" said another.
"Tickle the run and donkey!"
shouted the foreman.

What? No one understood what
anybody else said.

They became confused and grumpy. Soon the people stopped building the tower and the city altogether.

God used their confusion to make them live in different places, and there they raised families who spoke their own languages. (That's why there are thousands of different languages in the world.)

Plans fail when people work apart from God. No one is greater than He is.

Jesus Calling

"I am the vine; you are the branches. If a man remains in me and I in him, he will bear much fruit; apart from me you can do nothing."

JOHN 15:5

I am the Lord, the God and Creator of all things. I have given you gifts—making you able to build with your hands, run with your feet, and speak with your mouth. When you use these gifts in good ways because you love Me, you feel happy. I love seeing you enjoy what I have given you. But when you do things selfishly—apart from Me—it is not good for anyone.

I want you to live close to Me. Talk with Me often through your prayers. I am always listening.

God's Friend
Abram Follows God | from Genesis 12

Waiting is a really hard thing to do. When people want something or need something, they think, *Hurry, hurry!* It's easy to get tired of waiting.

God had a friend named Abram, and He told Abram to move to a land called Canaan. He also said, "Abram, I have a wonderful plan, and your family is a very important part of that plan. Through you, all the families on earth will be blessed. Follow Me and trust Me."

Abram knew that God would take care of them. So he and his wife packed their bags and followed God all the way to Canaan.

Then they waited for God to bless them with a family. And they waited. And waited some more.

God's Friend
God's Promise | from Genesis 15; 17–18

God had said Abram's family would be very important, but how could that be if he had no children? Abram and Sarai, his wife, were getting really old! And waiting was very hard. One night, God called him outside and said, "Abram, can you count all the stars?"

"Of course not!" Abram said. "There are too many." Millions and millions of stars were shining like diamonds in the black night.

"That is how many great-grandchildren you will have," God promised. And Abram believed God.

God came to Abram again, and this time He gave Abram a new name, Abraham, which means "father of many." Sarai's new name would be Sarah, and God said, "Soon you and Sarah will have a son."

Again Abraham believed, and he felt so happy that he laughed out loud. When Sarah heard, she laughed too, but for another reason: Sarah thought God's promise was impossible.

"We are too old to have babies," she said.

Jesus Calling

Jesus looked at them and said,
"With man this is impossible, but not with God;
all things are possible with God."

MARK 10:27

Believe in Me. Trust Me, and I will show you
how much I can do. Even when things seem impossible,
you can trust Me to do what I say I will do.
Nothing is too hard for Me!

God's Friend
Isaac Is Born | from Genesis 21

The following year, something wonderful happened: Sarah gave birth to a baby boy. The wait was over.

They named him Isaac, which means "he laughs." Sarah said, "God has brought me laughter, and whoever hears about this will laugh with me. Who would have thought we would have a child at our age?"

She was ninety years old, and Abraham was a hundred! Yet Abraham's family became so big that today—thousands of years later—people all over the world still remember him as Father Abraham, God's friend who had great faith.

Many years later, God would send one of Abraham's great-great-great- (plus a whole bunch more greats!) grandchildren, Jesus, to save His people from their sins. Jesus would show the whole world just how much God loves His children.

God's Friend
God Tests Abraham | from Genesis 22

When Isaac was older, God decided to test Abraham's faith. So He asked Abraham for a sacrifice, a big one. "Give Isaac back to Me, to live with Me in heaven."

Abraham had waited so long for a son. He loved Isaac, but he loved God more. So with a sad heart, Abraham agreed.

Abraham and Isaac climbed a mountain and met God there. "God," Abraham said with tears in his eyes, "if You want my only son, here he is."

God was pleased that Abraham loved and trusted Him enough to give Isaac back. He was so pleased that He told Abraham he didn't have to give Isaac back after all—God would accept a male sheep instead. God provided that sheep, and Abraham and Isaac were very happy about it!

God blessed Abraham for trusting Him so much. One day, God would sacrifice His own Son, Jesus, as a special Gift to the world.

Jesus Calling

And the scripture was fulfilled that says, "Abraham believed God, and it was credited to him as righteousness," and he was called God's friend.

JAMES 2:23

I want My children to know they can trust Me. Always. With all things. Trusting Me shows that you are My friend. I will take care of you, and I will be the best Friend you could ever have. Believe that I love you—because I do!

Jacob, a Man with Two Names

Jacob and Esau | from Genesis 25

Isaac grew up and married a lady named Rebekah. They had twin boys, Jacob and Esau. Esau was born first. He was all red and hairy. As the oldest boy, Esau would someday get most of his father's things and a special blessing. Jacob was born hanging on to Esau's heel.

When they grew up, quiet Jacob enjoyed staying home. Esau liked being outdoors and hunting wild animals. One day, Esau came home really hungry. Jacob had made a big bowl of stew. "Give me some of that!" Esau said. "I'm starving."

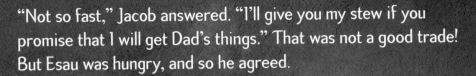

"Not so fast," Jacob answered. "I'll give you my stew if you promise that I will get Dad's things." That was not a good trade! But Esau was hungry, and so he agreed.

When Isaac grew old and it was time to give Esau the blessing, Jacob was tricky. Jacob disguised himself as his brother and covered his arms with furry animal skins so he would feel hairy. Because Isaac could not see well, he gave Jacob the blessing that should have gone to Esau.

Esau was very, very angry when he found out his brother had gotten their dad's things *and* his blessing.

Jacob, a Man with Two Names

Jacob's Dream | from Genesis 28

Because Esau was so angry, Jacob was afraid Esau would kill him, so Jacob ran away from his family. One night, when he was sleeping outside, Jacob dreamed about a stairway reaching all the way to heaven, with angels climbing up and down. In the dream, God made a promise to Jacob just like the one He had made to Jacob's grandfather Abraham. "I will give you the land you are sleeping on. You will have many children. The whole world will be blessed because of you and your relatives."

When Jacob woke up, he made a promise to God in return. "You will always be my God," he said. "And I will give back one tenth of everything You give to me."

God promised to take care of Jacob wherever he went.

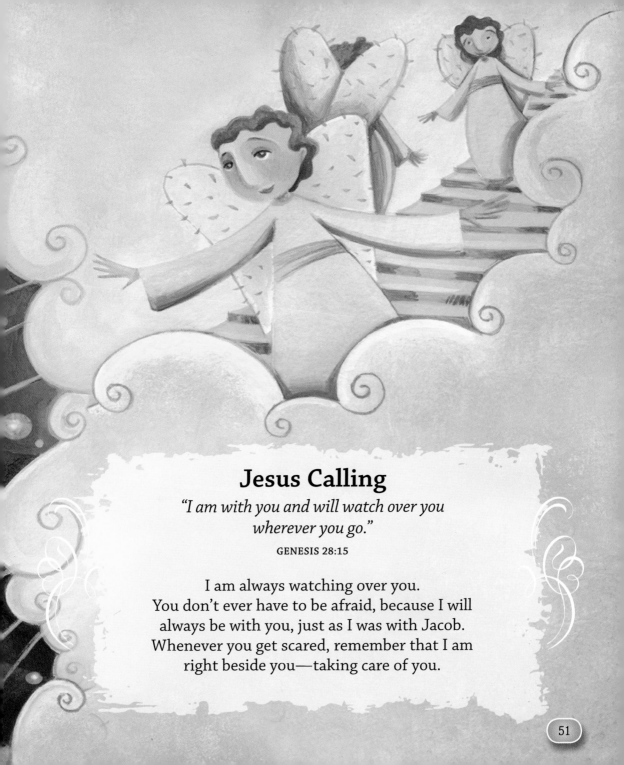

Jesus Calling

"I am with you and will watch over you wherever you go."

GENESIS 28:15

I am always watching over you.
You don't ever have to be afraid, because I will always be with you, just as I was with Jacob.
Whenever you get scared, remember that I am right beside you—taking care of you.

Jacob, a Man with Two Names

A New Name for Jacob | from Genesis 29; 32; 35

Jacob had two wives, Rachel and Leah. He loved Rachel, but just as he had tricked others in the past, he was tricked into marrying Leah.

God did not forget about Leah. He made her a big part of His great plan. She had eleven children, and through the line of her son Judah, Jesus would someday be born.

Jacob and his wives had thirteen children—one girl and twelve boys.

Dinner was very interesting with thirteen children . . .

"Move over!"

"Stop touching me!"

"That's my food! Give it back!"

God continued to be faithful to Jacob and his great big, noisy family. He decided to give Jacob a new name: Israel.

Jesus Calling

The word of the LORD is right and true;
he is faithful in all he does.

PSALM 33:4

Everything changes except for Me.
I am the same forever, and I never break My promises.
I will always be faithful to you, just as I was to Jacob.
I want you to learn about Me and believe My promises.
I am faithful; I won't let you down!

Joseph the Dreamer
Joseph and His Brothers | from Genesis 37

Joseph was one of Jacob's thirteen children. Joseph's older brothers disliked him because he tattled. They disliked him even more when their father gave Joseph a colorful new robe. They *really* disliked him when Joseph said, "I had a dream. We were tying bundles of grain, and your bundles bowed down to mine, like I was your king."

"Our king?" his brothers wailed. "No way!"

"I had another dream," Joseph said. "The sun, moon, and stars bowed down to me!"

One day, Joseph went to check on his brothers in the fields. When they saw him, they said, "We'll get rid of that dreamer who thinks he's so great." Then they grabbed Joseph and threw him into a well.

Later, a group of traders came along riding on camels.
"Where are you going?" the brothers asked.

"To Egypt," the men said.

So Joseph's brothers sold him to the traders. "We'll mess up
Joseph's new robe and tell Dad that a wild animal killed him,"
the brothers decided.

And that's what they did.

Joseph the Dreamer
Joseph and Potiphar's Wife | from Genesis 39

The traders sold Joseph as a slave to the captain of the king's guard, a man named Potiphar. With God's favor, Joseph did well at his work. He grew strong and handsome, so handsome that Potiphar's wife fell in love with him. "Come with me," she said.

"No!" Joseph cried. "That would be wrong; you are married!" From then on, Joseph tried to stay away from her.

Potiphar's wife felt angry because Joseph didn't obey her command. When no one was watching, she took Joseph's coat. Then she brought it to her husband. "Look! Joseph came to me to shame me," she lied.

So Potiphar threw Joseph into the king's prison. But God was with Joseph. Soon Joseph was put in charge of all the prisoners and all the prison work.

Jesus Calling

Even if you should suffer for what is right, you are blessed. "Do not fear what they fear; do not be frightened."

1 PETER 3:14

Sometimes in this world, you will have to suffer for doing the right thing—as Joseph did. Do not be afraid even then, for I am always with you. Call on Me, and I will comfort you. I can bring good even out of the bad things other people do.

Joseph the Dreamer
Joseph Is Set Free | from Genesis 40–41

God understands our dreams. While Joseph was in prison, God allowed him to understand dreams too. The king's wine taster got into trouble and was put in prison. The man asked Joseph to explain a dream. Joseph said, "Your dream means that you will get out of prison in three days. When that happens, ask the king if he will let me out too."

Joseph was right. The man was set free. But he forgot to tell the king about Joseph until . . .

Two years later!

The king of Egypt had a dream, and he asked the wine taster to explain it. "I cannot," the man said, "but I remember a young man from prison who can." So the king sent for Joseph, and Joseph explained his dream.

"Amazing!" the king said. "The Spirit of God is in this man." Then the king set Joseph free. In fact, he was so impressed that he put Joseph in charge of the whole land of Egypt.

Joseph the Dreamer
Joseph Forgives His Brothers | from Genesis 42–47

A great famine spread through the land. No one could find food. Back in Canaan, Joseph's family was starving. "We're so hungry!" they wailed.

By then, Joseph was governor of Egypt, and Egypt had lots of grain stored up because of his wise leadership. People came from all over to get some. Joseph's brothers came too. Not knowing what had become of Joseph, they didn't recognize him when they bowed to him—he was all grown up! But Joseph knew them.

"Oh, Governor, sir. May we please have some grain?" they asked.

After all those years! Joseph's brothers were before him and did not even know who he was.

Are they still the mean brothers who sold me into slavery? Joseph wondered. He questioned and tested them many times to see if they had changed.

They had! Finally, Joseph cried, "I am your brother Joseph!"

They were shocked speechless. They'd been so cruel those many years ago, and now Joseph was a mighty and powerful ruler. What would happen to them now?

They didn't need to worry. Joseph forgave them.

Though the brothers' plan was for evil—to harm Joseph—God had turned it into good. Because Joseph was in Egypt and in charge of storing up food, God made sure Joseph's whole family was saved from the famine. They all moved to Egypt, and when Jacob arrived, Joseph came to greet him and threw his arms around his father. They wept tears of joy because God had brought them together again.

Jesus Calling

Put up with each other, and forgive anyone
who does you wrong, just as Christ has forgiven you.

COLOSSIANS 3:13 CEV

Life is not always fair. When people do things that hurt
you, I want you to forgive them, remembering that
I always forgive you. I had to pay a very big price so I could
forgive you and others who trust Me as Savior. When you
forgive someone who has hurt you, this makes Me happy.
It will make you happy too.

61

The Story of Moses
A Baby in a Basket from Exodus 1–2

Jacob's family lived in Egypt for about 400 years after he died. His family kept growing and growing! Moms, dads, babies, big kids, grandmas and grandpas, aunts, uncles, cousins. Even though they all lived in Egypt, they called themselves Israelites (remember Jacob's new name?). They were God's people.

Egypt had a new king—a mean king. He hated the Israelites and made them his slaves. He planned to kill all their baby boys so Jacob's family would get smaller instead of bigger.

To protect her new baby boy, one mother made a basket that would float. She hid him in the basket in the reeds along the banks of the Nile River. The baby's sister watched to see what would happen.

The king's daughter was on the riverbank that day and saw him floating in his basket. "How sweet you are!" the princess cooed. She felt sorry for the baby, and she adopted him. She named him Moses, which means "I lifted him out of the water."

The Story of Moses
God Speaks to Moses | from Exodus 2–3

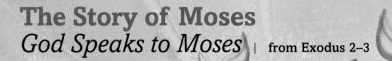

Even though Moses grew up in the palace of the king of Egypt, he knew he was an Israelite. One day he killed an Egyptian who was hurting a fellow Israelite. That made the king mad. Moses was afraid and ran away.

God knew how badly the king treated the slaves. He didn't like it one bit. And He was ready to do something about it.

While Moses tended some sheep out in the desert, he saw a bush on fire, but the bush didn't burn up. Moses went closer to see.

"Moses! Moses!" God called from the bush. Moses could not believe God was speaking to him. "Take off your sandals, Moses, for you are standing on holy ground. It is I, the God of Abraham, Isaac, and Jacob. I know that the king treats My people badly. Tell them that I will save them. Tell them that I sent you. Then go to the king and say, 'Let My people go.'"

God was sending him back to Egypt? Didn't God know that Moses had run away? Didn't God know that he was scared?

God knew all these things, but He had big plans for Moses. So Moses obeyed God. He and his brother, Aaron, went to see the king.

The Story of Moses
The Passover | from Exodus 5–12

Moses and Aaron told the king, "God says, 'Let My people go.'"
The king answered, "No." They said it again. The king said no again.
After that, the king was *really* mean to the slaves.

God had decided to punish the people of Egypt. But He also wanted
to show that He was much greater than the gods of Egypt. So God
sent ten plagues: a stinky river, frogs everywhere, bugs on everyone,
flies in the air, dead farm animals, terrible sores, hailstorms, locusts,
total darkness, and . . .

The king still said, "No, I will not let your people go."

Then God said, "I will pass over the houses of Egypt, and death will come to all its firstborn sons and male animals." But He also told each Israelite family to kill a lamb and put some of the blood on the outside of their front door. This was to be a sign that they were God's children and that they wanted Him to save their sons and animals. Jesus would someday die like these lambs to save His children from being punished for their sins. That is why Jesus is called the Passover Lamb.

When God did as He had said, all of Egypt's firstborn sons and male animals died, including the king's own son. Then the king told Moses, "Gather your people and get out of here!"

Jesus Calling

Finally, be strong in the Lord and in his mighty power.
EPHESIANS 6:10

I made you to be strong and to do many things, but I want you to do things with My help. When you really trust Me, I can do more than you could ever imagine, just as I did for the children of Israel. My mighty Power is much, much greater than the power of all the strongest people in the world put together— including kings, presidents, and great athletes.

The Story of Moses

Moses the Great Leader | from Exodus 14–16

God led Moses and the Israelites out of Egypt.

Back in Egypt, the king was mad at himself: "What have I done? Where are my slaves? I should not have let the Israelites go free!" He ordered his army to go after them. Soldiers mounted their horses. The chariots came charging. Thousands of soldiers stormed with their weapons . . . all of them chasing God's people.

The Israelites saw that the Egyptian soldiers were coming, and they were afraid. In front of them lay the great Red Sea. "Pick up your staff, Moses," God said. "Hold it up toward the water." Moses obeyed. The wind rushed . . . the sea tore open . . . and a dry path appeared with walls of water on each side. God's people hurried through until every one of them reached the other side. The Egyptians were still chasing them when God slammed the sea shut, saving His people from the king's soldiers.

And the Israelites sang, "God is so great that He can make the sea part to save His people!"

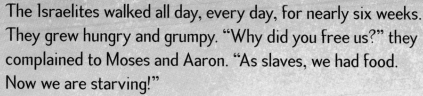

The Israelites walked all day, every day, for nearly six weeks. They grew hungry and grumpy. "Why did you free us?" they complained to Moses and Aaron. "As slaves, we had food. Now we are starving!"

God heard. He sent a flock of birds, known as quail, to the Israelites for their dinner. Then He told Moses, "Tomorrow, bread will rain down from heaven. Tell My people to gather it but to take only what they need for the day."

The next morning, the people saw something that looked like thin wafers all over the ground. "What is it?" they asked Moses.

"This is God's bread from heaven," he said. Every morning— except the day of rest—wherever they went, flakes of bread fell from heaven and covered the ground. The people called it *manna*. For forty years, as they walked through the desert, manna kept them from starving.

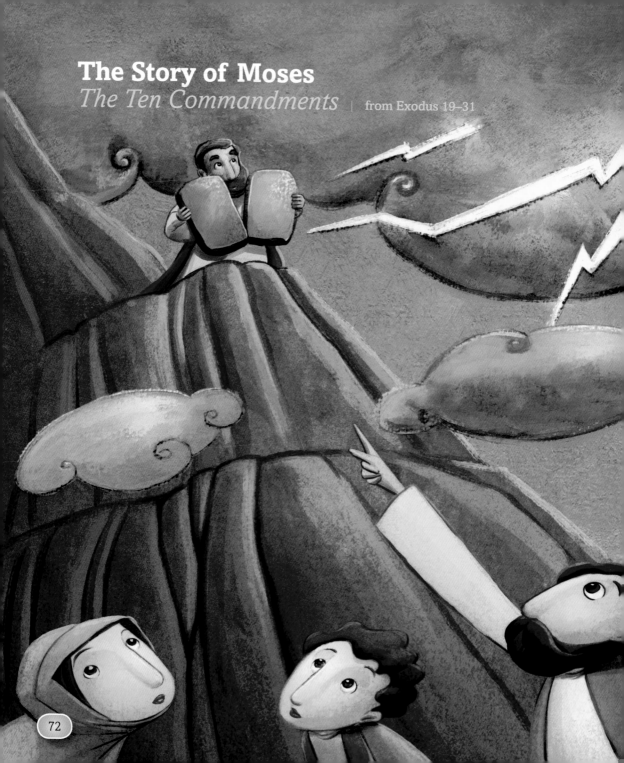

The Story of Moses
The Ten Commandments | from Exodus 19–31

God promised the Israelites a special place to live. But before they got there, God wanted them to understand His rules. God told Moses to meet Him on a mountaintop. So Moses went up and stayed there with God for forty days and nights, learning God's laws. God then took two big pieces of stone. On them, He carved the Ten Commandments—ten special rules for us to obey.

1. Make God your only god.
2. Don't worship anything except God.
3. Be respectful in using God's name.
4. Keep the Lord's day special.
5. Honor your parents.
6. Do not kill.
7. Keep your marriage promises.
8. Do not steal.
9. Do not lie.
10. Do not want what others already have.

Jesus Calling

"Keep my commands and follow them. I am the LORD."

LEVITICUS 22:31

I gave you My commands because I love you so much. When you follow them, you not only bring *Me* joy; you also make your *own* life full of joy. I know what is best for you because I made you— I put you together before you were born. I am your Creator!

The Story of Moses
A Golden Calf | from Exodus 32–33

When Moses was gone for so long on the mountain with God, the Israelites stopped trusting God. They said to Aaron, "We need a god who can lead us."

So Aaron told them to take off their gold jewelry. He melted the gold and molded it into the shape of a calf.

The people bowed to the golden calf and brought it gifts. They danced around and worshiped it.

God was really mad when he saw His people worshiping a statue. He sent Moses back down the mountain. "What have you done?" Moses cried out to Aaron. "Trust only God!"

Moses asked God to forgive the people. Though God punished them, He never stopped loving them. He told them to keep walking toward His Promised Land.

Jesus Calling

*"I wipe away your sins because of who I am.
And so, I will forget the wrongs you have done."*

ISAIAH 43:25 CEV

When you do something wrong, remember that I still love you. Just come to Me and tell Me you're sorry. Because you are My precious child, nothing can stop Me from loving you. I will forget the wrong things you have done, and I'll help you do right things.

Spies! | from Numbers 13–14

Moses picked twelve of his finest men and told them, "Go. Spy on our enemies. Sneak into the land God promised us, and report back. Find out if the people are powerful or weak. Tell us about their cities and land. If you can, bring back some fruit."

The men did what Moses said and spied on Canaan for forty days.

They brought back bunches of grapes that were so big it took two men to carry them! "The land is good for growing food, but the cities have thick walls, and the people there are giants! They are so big and strong that they make us look like grasshoppers."

One of the spies, Caleb, jumped up. "Hey! Those big guys shouldn't scare us! God is with us! Let's go take our land from these people. They believe in false gods and serve idols."

His friend Joshua agreed. "Let's do it!"

Their faith pleased God, but the other ten spies were afraid. The trip from Egypt to the Promised Land should have taken eleven days, but because the people did not trust in God, they had to wander in the desert for forty long years!

Only Joshua, Caleb, and the youngest of the Israelites would get to go into the Promised Land.

Jesus Calling

Do not be afraid of [your enemies];
the LORD your God himself will fight for you.

DEUTERONOMY 3:22

I know the world is scary sometimes. Many people are bigger than you, and it's easy to be afraid. But remember, I will fight for you. So you can be brave by trusting Me. I'll be pleased with you—just as I was with Joshua and Caleb. When you feel afraid, say, "I trust You, Jesus."

Joshua and the Walls of Jericho | from Joshua 2

In the Promised Land was the great city of Jericho. Joshua, the new leader of the Israelites, sent two men to spy on Jericho to figure out how they could take over the city. Did they need a great battle? Would swords and spears work? Maybe a sneaky invasion?
The spies hid in the house of a woman named Rahab. When Jericho's king heard they were there, he sent messengers to Rahab's place. "Send those spies outside!" the men demanded.

But Rahab said, "They've already left. Run. You might catch them."

The messengers went away to find the spies.

The spies were on Rahab's roof, hiding under a pile of grain.
"I heard that God gave you Jericho," Rahab said. "The people
are afraid of your God and worry that a big fight will happen here.
I've helped you, so will you help me? Promise that God will
keep me and my family safe."

After the spies promised, Rahab used a bright red rope to
help them climb to the ground.

"When the big fight comes, stay inside with your family,"
the spies said. "Tie this red rope in your window, and you will
be safe." So that's what Rahab did.

"Armor ready! March!" Joshua and his army went to take Jericho. But the city's gates were locked. Its people wouldn't give up without a fight.

God told Joshua, "March around Jericho's walls one time today. Take along seven priests with seven trumpets, but tell them not to play. Do this every day for six days. On the seventh day, march around seven times. The last time, have the priests sound the trumpets. Then everybody shout."

Those instructions seemed crazy! That was not how Joshua expected to win a battle. But Joshua obeyed God. "Forward march!" he yelled. Around the walls they went—the army, the priests, and Joshua.

On day seven, they marched around the walls seven times. On the seventh time, *Ta-ta-dah*, the trumpets wailed. "Shout!" Joshua yelled. Jericho's walls came tumbling down. The army rushed in and took over the city.

Remember Rahab? She and her family were safe during the big battle of Jericho. She became the great-great-grandma of King David, and Jesus would be born from her family line too.

Jesus Calling

Children, you belong to the Lord, and you do
the right thing when you obey your parents.
EPHESIANS 6:1 CEV

Joshua followed My instructions even though
they seemed very strange. He understood that I know
best, and he trusted Me. You are My child,
and I want you to obey Me. I also want you to obey
your parents because this is the right thing to do.

Gideon's Little Army | from Judges 6–7

The Israelites did it again: They forgot about God. And things soon went wrong. This time, they lost their land to a powerful enemy, the Midianites. "Help us!" they cried out to God. So God sent an angel to a young man named Gideon. Now, Gideon was not considered an important ruler; he was just a worker threshing wheat. But God had an important message for him. "Gideon!" He said. "Go save My people."

"Who? Me?" Gideon answered. "I'm just a weakling."

"I chose you," God said. "And I will be with you."

Gideon wanted a big army to fight the Midianites. But God allowed him only 300 men. Imagine: 300 men to fight 135,000 powerful soldiers! Still, Gideon trusted God.

Each soldier had a trumpet and a clay jar with a torch inside. One night, Gideon's army surrounded the enemy camp. They blew their trumpets, smashed the jars, and held up the torches. "For the Lord!" they shouted.

This confused the Midianites. "Let's get out of here!" they said and ran far, far away. Through a "weakling" named Gideon, God gave the Israelites their land back.

Jesus Calling

For when I am weak, then I am strong.

2 CORINTHIANS 12:10 NKJV

Even though Gideon thought of himself as weak,
I used him in a very powerful way.
My Strength works best in weakness.
So don't try to be strong in yourself. Trust *Me*,
and let My Power show through your weakness.

Samson the Strong Guy | from Judges 14–16

How strong was Samson? Samson was so strong that he could lift a lion or tear open iron gates or kill a gang of bad guys. Unfortunately, the Israelites' super-strong leader was more interested in serving himself than God. He led God's people at a time when they fought another enemy—the Philistines. The Philistines hated Samson. They wanted to kill him, but they were afraid. "Maybe his girlfriend, Delilah, can find out what makes him so strong," they said. Delilah was a Philistine, so she agreed to help.

When they were alone, Delilah asked, "Samson, what makes you so strong?" But Samson wouldn't tell her. "Please, honey?" she coaxed. Delilah kept asking and asking until Samson finally gave in.

"It's my long hair," he grumbled. "I am weak without it." Then he fell asleep.

While he slept, Delilah had someone cut his hair. After that, she yelled, "The Philistines are coming!" Samson awoke, and his enemies grabbed him. Without his hair, he was too weak to fight. The Philistines made Samson blind. Then they threw him into prison.

The Philistines worshiped a fish-man god they called Dagon. They had a party in their temple to honor this false god, and Samson was the entertainment. However, Samson had repented—told God he was sorry—and his hair had grown back. This gave him supernatural strength again. As thousands of Philistines watched, Samson said to himself, *All of the Philistine leaders are here. I know how to get back at them for blinding me . . . but it will cost me my life.*

Samson decided it was worth it. He stood between two thick pillars in the center of the temple. "Please, God," he prayed. "Give me strength. Let me with one shove get revenge on the Philistines." Then Samson pushed the pillars as hard as he could, smashing them to bits. The temple crashed down, killing Samson and all the Philistine leaders.

God to the rescue again! This time He used Samson, who was not even a very good man, to save His people from their enemy.

Jesus Calling

If anybody does sin, we have one who speaks to the Father in our defense—Jesus Christ, the Righteous One.

1 JOHN 2:1

Samson spent much of his life living apart from Me. In the end, he came back to Me, and I forgave him. When you do something that makes you feel far away from Me, come to Me and tell Me you're sorry. Because you are My child, I will forgive you. I want you to live close to Me.

Ruth and Naomi

from The Book of Ruth

Wait for me!" Ruth begged her mother-in-law, Naomi. "I'll go with you. Your God will be my God, and I will never leave you." Ruth was as beautiful on the inside as she was on the outside. Her husband and his brother—Naomi's sons—had died. Naomi's husband had died too. So Naomi decided to go back to where she used to live. Ruth would not let her go alone. So the two women traveled many miles to Bethlehem, Naomi's homeland.

When they got there, Ruth and Naomi were too poor to buy food. They lived on leftover grain that Ruth found in fields that belonged to Naomi's wealthy relative, a man named Boaz. When Boaz saw Ruth gathering grain, he invited her to lunch. "It's wonderful that you are so kind to Naomi," Boaz said. "May God repay you for your kindness." Before Ruth left, Boaz made sure she had plenty of food to share with Naomi.

When Ruth came home with all that food, Naomi said, "God bless Boaz! He is my husband's close relative. He will take care of us."

Then Naomi had an idea; she thought it would be good if Boaz married Ruth. Boaz thought it was a good idea too!

Ruth and Boaz got married and had a baby boy. They named him Obed. His grandmother, Naomi, loved him, and he loved her back. When Obed grew up, he had a son, and later, his son had a son. And that little boy grew up to be a mighty king named David.

Isn't God great? He rewarded Ruth's kindness and turned Naomi's sad life into something good. God used people from different countries, like Ruth and Rahab, in His plan to help His children.

Jesus Calling

All things work together for good to those who love God.

ROMANS 8:28 NKJV

Everything that happens fits into My plan
for good if you love Me. Trust Me with big things,
like your friendships and future dreams.
You can also trust Me for little, everyday things.
Remember how I took care of Ruth and Naomi.
Nothing is too big or too small for Me.
So talk with Me about everything.

Hannah's Special Prayer

from 1 Samuel 1–2

Hannah begged God for a baby boy. She wanted a baby more than anything else. When she went to the temple (which is like a church), Hannah cried and prayed really hard. "God, if You give me a son, I will give him back to You to serve You."

A priest named Eli overheard. "May God give you what you have asked for," he said.

God heard Hannah's prayer and gave her a son. She named the baby Samuel. When Samuel was older, Hannah took him to live with Eli the priest. There Samuel learned to serve God. Hannah was never far away though. She loved her little boy; he was her special gift to God.

Hannah kept praising God, and because she was so faithful, God gave her more children. And Samuel? He grew up to be one of the greatest men in Israel.

Jesus Calling

Please listen, LORD! Answer my prayer for help.

PSALM 86:6 CEV

I love to hear your prayers. Come and tell Me what you want. I know just what you need, and I will answer your prayers. As you see Me work in your life, your faith in Me will grow stronger. Come to Me with a thankful heart, and trust Me to do what is best.

God Speaks to Samuel | from 1 Samuel 3

Young Samuel had almost drifted off to sleep when he heard, "Samuel? Samuel!"

Samuel ran to Eli's bedroom. "Yes, Eli?" he asked.

Poor Eli was sound asleep. "Go back to bed," the priest complained. So Samuel did.

He heard it again: "Samuel?"

"Here I am, Eli," Samuel said.

This happened three times, until Eli told him, "God is talking to you, Samuel. Stay in bed and listen!"

God *was* talking to Samuel. He had a special message for Samuel to give to Eli. "I'm listening, God," Samuel said.

"Eli's sons said and did bad things against Me," God told him. "Eli did nothing to stop them, so I will punish them for what they have done."

In the morning, Samuel told Eli everything God had said. All of Israel also heard that God had talked to Samuel and that Samuel had listened. God stayed close to Samuel, and Samuel loved and obeyed God as he grew up.

Jesus Calling

"You will seek Me and find Me,
when you search for Me with all your heart."
JEREMIAH 29:13 NKJV

You may not hear My voice out loud like Samuel did. But if you listen closely, you will hear Me in your heart. Find a quiet place and be still. I will speak to you softly and tenderly, saying, *I am with you.*
I am with you. I love you.

The Story of David
David, God's Chosen King | from 1 Samuel 16

As one of God's prophets, or messengers, Samuel kept on listening to God and telling people what God said. One day God told him, "Go to the little town of Bethlehem. You'll find a man there named Jesse. One of his sons will be My new choice for Israel's king. I will tell you which one when you meet them."

One by one, Jesse brought his sons to Samuel. The first was handsome. The next looked strong. *Surely one of these will be king,* Samuel thought.

But God said, "No. Looks do not matter to Me. I see what is in a man's heart."

Jesse brought five more sons to Samuel, and God said,
"No, no, no, no, and no!"

"Is that all of them?" Samuel asked.

"David, my youngest and smallest boy, is watching the sheep,"
Jesse said.

Samuel asked to meet him. In spite of his size, David was bright-
eyed, handsome, and strong.

"He is the one!" God said.

Many years later, another king would come from Bethlehem.
He would be from David's family line. He is the King
of all kings—Jesus Christ.

The Story of David
David and Goliath | from 1 Samuel 17

Remember the bad Philistines? Well, they wanted to fight the Israelites again. But they had a giant soldier—really, a giant. His name was Goliath. He was more than nine feet tall and wore a helmet and a coat of armor. He carried a huge spear. Every day, Goliath shouted at God's people, "Come on. Fight with me!" And Goliath yelled terrible things about God. The Israelite soldiers were terrified of him. Even their king, Saul, felt afraid. So God sent help—the young shepherd David.

"I'm not scared," David said. "Let me at him! God is on our side."

David wore no armor. He carried only a slingshot and a bag of stones, and he marched right up to Goliath.

"What's up, little guy?" the giant said.

David shouted back, "You may come with big weapons to fight us, but I come in the name of the Lord!" David put a stone in his slingshot, aimed it at Goliath's head, and fired.

"Ouch!" *THUD!* Goliath fell to the ground. Dead.

The Philistines ran away, with the Israelite army chasing them. God had rescued His people again—this time through David, a slingshot, and a stone.

The Story of David

David and Jonathan | from 1 Samuel 18–20

David became a great hero, and that made King Saul jealous. He hated David. Saul even threw a spear at David. *Twice!*

David and Saul's son Jonathan were best friends and as close as brothers. One day, Jonathan went to David and said, "Dad is so jealous he wants to kill you! You need to run from him. Hide in the field. I'll meet you there later."

Jonathan begged his father, King Saul, not to kill David, but Saul threw a spear at him too! Jonathan went to the field and found his friend. "Dad won't change his mind," Jonathan said. "You have to go far away, where you will be safe."

David hugged Jonathan and cried.

"Don't forget," Jonathan said, "we've promised God that we will be friends forever. Go now. Hurry, before Dad comes after you."

Jesus Calling

A friend loves at all times.

PROVERBS 17:17 NKJV

Best friends trust and love each other. They enjoy
being together. I want to be your closest Friend.
Spend time with Me and talk to Me.
I know everything about you—the best and the
worst. But I love you as if you were perfect.
That's because I'm not only your Friend;
I'm also your Savior.

The Story of David
David Spares Saul | from 1 Samuel 24

David went far away to a rocky place and hid in a cave. Meanwhile, King Saul and 3,000 of his soldiers were looking for David. One day, they came to the cave where David was hiding. Saul went into the cave, not knowing that David was inside. David crept quietly toward Saul and cut off a corner of his robe. Suddenly David felt ashamed for disrespecting the king. He came out, bowed to Saul, and said, "My master and king!"

"Why are you so mad at me?" David asked. "Look." He held up the piece of Saul's robe. "I could have killed you with my sword, but I didn't. God might punish you for what you are trying to do to me, but I won't hurt you."

Then Saul began to cry. "You *are* better than me," he said. "You repaid evil with good. You spared my life. Someday, David, you will be a great king."

And just as God had promised, David became a great king.

The Story of David
Poems, Songs, and Prayers | from Psalm 23; 100

King David liked to write poems, songs, and prayers called psalms to honor God.

Psalm 23 NLT

The LORD is my shepherd; I have all that I need. He lets me rest in green meadows; he leads me beside peaceful streams. He renews my strength. He guides me along right paths, bringing honor to his name.

Even when I walk through the darkest valley, I will not be afraid, for you are close beside me. Your rod and your staff protect and comfort me.

You prepare a feast for me in the presence of my enemies. You honor me by anointing my head with oil. My cup overflows with blessings. Surely your goodness and unfailing love will pursue me all the days of my life, and I will live in the house of the Lord forever.

David wrote psalms that praised and thanked God.

Psalm 100 CEV

Shout praises to the LORD, everyone on this earth. Be joyful and sing as you come in to worship the LORD!

You know the LORD is God! He created us, and we belong to him; we are his people, the sheep in his pasture.

Be thankful and praise the LORD as you enter his temple. The LORD is good! His love and faithfulness will last forever.

Jesus Calling

It is good to give thanks to the LORD, and to sing praises to Your name, O Most High.

PSALM 92:1 NKJV

Thanking Me brings you closer to Me.
Thank Me for all the good things in your life.
And when things don't go your way, praise Me anyway.
Spend lots of time praising and thanking Me.
This will make you feel happy.
And I will be pleased with you.

Solomon's Wisdom from 1 Kings 1–4

King David grew old, and it became time to anoint a new king. He chose his son Solomon. David felt proud watching Solomon sitting on his throne and leading God's people. Before he died, David gave Solomon instructions about how a king should behave and, more important, about loving God.

Solomon went to a holy place to worship God. The Lord spoke to him there in a dream. "Ask Me for anything you want," God said.

Solomon answered, "I want to be a good and fair king. Please give me wisdom so I will make the right decisions."

God was happy that Solomon had asked for wisdom instead of riches or greatness. "I will make you wiser than anyone who has ever lived," God said. He gave Solomon wisdom, wealth, and respect. King Solomon became so wise that people from all over the world traveled to his palace just to hear him.

Jesus Calling

Trust in the LORD with all your heart,
and do not lean on your own understanding.

PROVERBS 3:5 ESV

I gave Solomon the gift of wisdom so that
he could do what was right. When he trusted in Me,
he was very wise. If you spend time reading your
Bible and praying to Me, this will help you
trust Me and do right things.

Patient Job | from The Book of Job

Job was a very blessed man. He had a wife and many children. He had lots of land and cattle and helpers. But Job's life was truly blessed because he loved and worshiped God.

Satan told God, "Job only loves You because of all You've done for him. Without them, he would turn from You." God allowed Satan to take Job's land, animals, helpers, and even his children. Still, Job worshiped God.

"Let me cover Job's body with painful sores," Satan said. "Then he will turn from You." So God allowed it. Job felt sad and miserable. But still, he trusted God.

Job's friends asked, "What did you do wrong for God to punish you like this?" Yet Job hadn't sinned.

His wife said, "You'd be better off dead." Yet as bad as he felt, he still believed in God and waited patiently for Him to act.

Finally, God spoke. He reminded Job of His wonderful creation. He scolded Job's friends for giving Job bad advice. Then, as a reward for Job's faithfulness, God gave back everything that Satan had taken—and more! Job lived 140 years, and he praised God every day.

Jesus Calling

I waited patiently for the LORD;
he turned to me and heard my cry.

PSALM 40:1

Everyone has problems. Satan is your enemy, and he will try to make you turn away from Me—especially when you are hurting. The best praise you can give Me is to trust Me when you're having a hard time. Talk to Me about your problems, and I will help you with them. Also, I will give you My Peace.

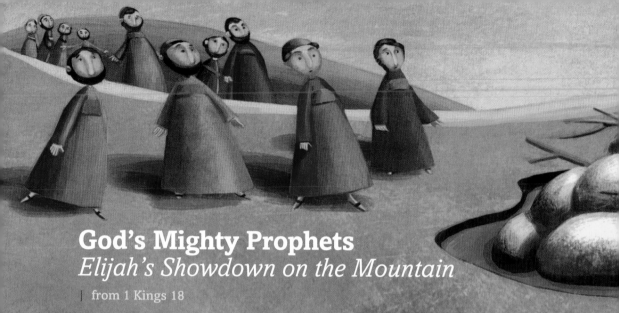

God's Mighty Prophets
Elijah's Showdown on the Mountain
| from 1 Kings 18

Queen Jezebel and King Ahab were bullies! They were mean, mean, mean. The bad king and queen got the Israelites to stop trusting God and start worshiping an idol named Baal. They even killed some of God's prophets. But the prophet Elijah trusted God with all his heart.

"I will prove that my God is the only real God. Let's have a contest," he said. "You priests of Baal can offer a sacrifice to your god, and I'll offer a sacrifice to mine. The One True God will send fire from heaven to burn up the altar wood."

All the Israelites came to watch. Baal's priests went first. "Send fire, Baal!" they shouted. But nothing happened.

"What's wrong?" Elijah asked. "Is Baal sleeping? Is he busy?" Elijah laid his sacrifice on the altar. To prove that he wasn't doing anything tricky, he asked the people to soak it with water. Then Elijah prayed, "Please, God, send fire to show that You are the only true God."

Zap! Fire whooshed down from heaven and burned up the wet altar and Elijah's sacrifice. The Israelites fell down and worshiped God.

Jesus Calling

Who is this King of glory? The LORD strong and mighty, the LORD mighty in battle.

PSALM 24:8

When you need My help, call out to Me. I will answer you. I'm never too busy for you, and I'm never asleep. I will do great and wonderful things to show how much I love you. I am strong and mighty! I can take good care of you.

God's Mighty Prophets
Elisha and the Chariots of Fire | from 2 Kings 6

Someone always wanted to take the Promised Land away from God's people. This time it was the Syrians. They started a big fight, and the Israelites might have been killed if God hadn't used Elisha.

The enemy soldiers surrounded Elisha's town. But Elisha saw something they couldn't: God's angel army was there too. Fiery horses and flaming chariots dashed around. Then, *POP!* God blinded the Syrian soldiers.

"You're in the wrong town," Elisha said, tricking them. "Come on. Let's go find Elisha."

Elisha marched the soldiers straight to the king of Israel, and the king wanted to kill them. "Don't," Elisha said. "Feed them a big dinner and set them free." In this way, Elisha taught the enemy about God's power and mercy.

Jesus Calling

"Now this is eternal life: that they may know you, the only true God, and Jesus Christ, whom you have sent."

JOHN 17:3

I am the One True God. Even though you cannot see Me, you can trust that I am always with you. Call on Me as Elijah and Elisha did, and I will bless you in many ways. Knowing Me is the most important thing in the whole world!

God's Mighty Prophets
Jonah and the Big Fish | from The Book of Jonah

God said to Jonah, "I want you to go to Nineveh and tell its people to shape up and follow Me." Nineveh was a really sinful town, and Jonah thought he and his people were better than the bullies of Nineveh. Jonah did not want to help these people, so instead of obeying God, he bought a ticket on a ship and sailed away.

No one can run away from God because God sees everything. And God saw Jonah.

God sent a fierce storm out to the sea. Waves pounded the ship and rocked it to and fro. "Help us!" the sailors begged their false gods, but nothing happened. Then one of them remembered Jonah. "Hey, you. Call on your God."

"It's my fault," Jonah admitted. "God is angry. Throw me overboard, and the sea will calm down."

The sailors were afraid to harm him, but the storm got so bad that they threw Jonah overboard. Then the storm went away.

Lord, help me," Jonah prayed as he sank down, down, down to the ocean's bottom. As soon as he said it, along came a big, hungry fish . . . and *GULP!* Jonah slid past its teeth and into its tummy. There, Jonah told God he was sorry, and he praised God for saving his life. "Some people turn from You and worship false gods," he said, "but not me. I promise to sing praises to You because I know that You are the only One who can save me." But Jonah still did not want to see God help the people in Nineveh.

Jonah was trapped inside the fish. After three days, the fish's tummy began to turn somersaults, tossing Jonah round and round. With a big heave-ho, the fish threw up and spit Jonah out on the beach, safe and sound.

God sent a fish to save Jonah from the sea, and Jonah was in the tummy of that fish for three days and three nights. Many years later, Jesus would be dead and in a grave for three days, but He would come back to life again on the third day.

Jonah knew that running away from what God wanted him to do was wrong. After the big fish spit him out, he decided to go and tell the people of Nineveh that their city would be destroyed in forty days if they didn't turn to God. The people listened to Jonah and believed. They repented, feeling sad about all the bad things they had done and telling God they were sorry. So God did not punish them.

Jonah was angry that God would forgive the people of Nineveh. He thought they should be punished. So God had to teach Jonah to love all people, even if they have done some bad things.

Jesus Calling

Show me Your ways, O LORD; teach me Your paths.

PSALM 25:4 NKJV

Some people—like Jonah—try to run away from Me instead of obeying Me. But I am everywhere, and I know everything. So trying to run away from Me is silly—and it is wrong. Try to live as close to Me as you can. I will teach you many things and show you the right way to go.

God's Mighty Prophets
Isaiah Meets God | from Isaiah 6–9

It's a big deal to meet a king. You can imagine how nervous Isaiah felt when God, the greatest King, the Lord All-Powerful, allowed him to peek into heaven.

In the Bible, Isaiah tells us what he saw: "God sat on a high throne. The edges of His robe filled the whole temple. Fiery creatures with six wings surrounded Him, and they flew about saying, 'Holy, holy is our God! Earth is filled with His glory.'"

God had a special mission for Isaiah: He was to tell the people they were sinning. If they did not repent and change their ways, they would lose their country and their freedom.

Later, God gave Isaiah another message. This message was about God's mercy and His plan for the salvation of His people.

> For to us a child is born,
>   to us a son is given,
>   and the government will be on his shoulders.
> And he will be called
>   Wonderful Counselor, Mighty God,
>   Everlasting Father, Prince of Peace. (Isaiah 9:6)

God would send Jesus, the Rescuer, to free His people from sin.

Jesus Calling

"For the Son of Man came to seek and to save the lost."

LUKE 19:10 ESV

I have many names: Wonderful Counselor, Mighty God, Everlasting Father, Prince of Peace, Son of God, Jesus . . . I came to save the world from sin. Call Me by any of My names, and I will hear you. I will save you from your sins. Then, someday we will live together forever in heaven. I promise.

God's Prophet Daniel | from Daniel 2

The Israelites disobeyed God so much that they got into a lot of trouble. A very powerful king named Nebuchadnezzar brought his huge army and took the Israelites away from the Promised Land.

King Nebuchadnezzar had nightmares. He deserved them, too, after capturing the Israelites and stealing their land. He kept dreaming about a giant statue, and none of his magicians could explain what it meant.

"I can help," said a prisoner named Daniel. "No human can tell what your dream means, but God can." Then God described to Daniel the king's scary dream, and Daniel explained the king's dream exactly like God told him.

"That's right!" the king smiled. "That's my dream!"

"You are the statue's head," Daniel said. "And a big stone falls from a mountain and smashes the statue to bits."

King Nebuchadnezzar's smile turned to a frown.

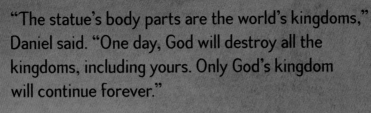

"The statue's body parts are the world's kingdoms," Daniel said. "One day, God will destroy all the kingdoms, including yours. Only God's kingdom will continue forever."

Jesus is the King of that forever kingdom. The king fell to the ground and worshiped. "Now I know," he said, "that your God is the only God."

Finally, the evil king understood. Or did he?

Shadrach, Meshach, and Abednego

| from Daniel 3

It didn't take long before King Nebuchadnezzar forgot about the only true God. He had a huge statue made from gold. Then he made a very bad rule. "Nations and peoples of every language, this is what you are commanded to do: As soon as you hear the sound of musical instruments such as the horn, flute, harp, and pipe, you must fall down and worship the image of gold. Whoever refuses will immediately be thrown into a blazing furnace."

No one wanted to be thrown into a fiery furnace. So when the music played, the people bowed down and worshiped the statue—except for Shadrach, Meshach, and Abednego. These men loved God, and there was no way they would worship the king's golden statue.

"You have one chance," the king warned them. "When the music plays, either you bow, or into the furnace you go. We'll see what your God does then."

"Our God is able to save us from that furnace, but even if He doesn't, we will serve Him anyway," the men said. This made the king hopping mad, and he ordered the furnace to be made seven times hotter.

The king's men threw Shadrach, Meshach, and Abednego into the blazing furnace. But the king couldn't believe his eyes. "Didn't you throw three men into the fire?" he asked.

"Yes, Your Majesty," his men answered.

"I see four men in there, and none of them is harmed." The king went nearer the furnace. "Shadrach, Meshach, and Abednego, come out!" he shouted.

Out they came, perfectly fine. Not one hair on their heads was burned because Jesus had been with them inside the furnace. The king said, "Praise be to the One True God. I decree that the people of all nations shall not say anything bad about the God of Shadrach, Meshach, and Abednego."

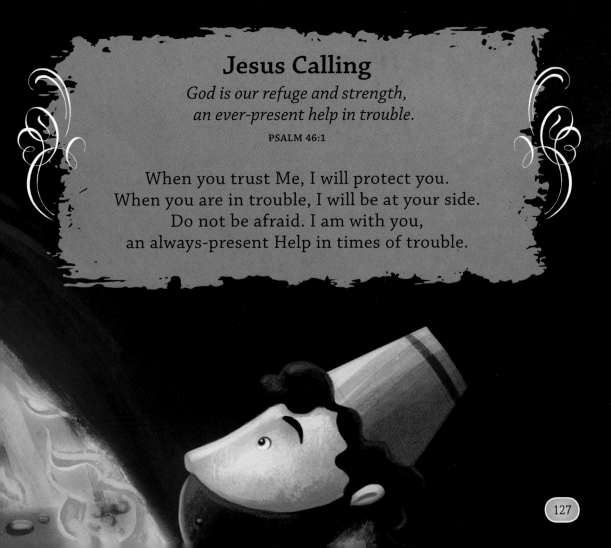

Jesus Calling

God is our refuge and strength,
an ever-present help in trouble.

PSALM 46:1

When you trust Me, I will protect you.
When you are in trouble, I will be at your side.
Do not be afraid. I am with you,
an always-present Help in times of trouble.

Daniel and the Lions' Den | from Daniel 6

Daniel was a wise and good worker, and the new king rewarded him with an important job: He put Daniel in charge of all the kingdom's governors. Well, the governors didn't like this one bit! They hated Daniel because he was the king's favorite.

"We have to do something to make Daniel look bad," one of them said.

"He won't worship anyone other than his God," said another.

"Maybe we can use that against him." So the governors made a terrible, evil plan. But for it to work, they needed to trick the king.

"Your Majesty," they said. "You are so wonderful that we think you should honor yourself. Make a law that everyone in the kingdom must worship you and no one else for the next thirty days. If someone disobeys, he should be thrown to the lions."

"What a great idea!" the king said. So he made the law and signed it.

When Daniel heard this, he refused to obey. He went to his room, knelt by the window, and prayed to God like he always did. The governors saw what Daniel did, and they tattled to the king.

"You made the law, and it cannot be changed," the men told the king. The king liked Daniel, and he did not want to hurt him. But a law is a law. So he ordered Daniel to be thrown into a pit of roaring lions. The pit was then sealed with a stone. All night long the king worried and hoped that Daniel's God could save him.

At daybreak the king got up and ran to the pit. "Daniel!" he shouted. "Did your God save you?"

"Yes!" Daniel answered. "God sent an angel to protect me. He kept the lions from eating me."

The king was so happy. He let Daniel out of the pit and then sent this message to all the people: "I command everyone in my kingdom to worship and honor the God of Daniel. His power and His kingdom will last forever."

In this way, many people from different countries came to know about the True God.

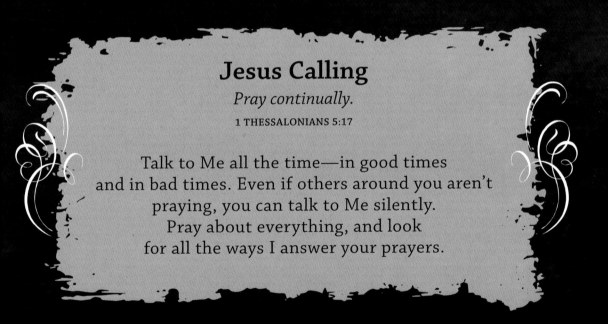

Jesus Calling

Pray continually.

1 THESSALONIANS 5:17

Talk to Me all the time—in good times and in bad times. Even if others around you aren't praying, you can talk to Me silently. Pray about everything, and look for all the ways I answer your prayers.

Beautiful Queen Esther | from Esther 2–8

A new country had come to power, and the Israelites had to live under the rule of King Xerxes of Persia.

King Xerxes wanted a wife, and from among the most beautiful girls in Persia he chose Esther. Esther was a poor girl, but she was as smart as she was pretty. She was everything the king wanted. But Esther also had a secret. She was an Israelite, and her cousin Mordecai was the Israelites' leader. If the king found out, he might not want to marry her.

"Marry the king," Mordecai said. "But keep it a secret that you are an Israelite. The Persians don't like us."

On her wedding day, Esther felt like the most beautiful princess. The king placed a crown on her head, and in her honor he held a banquet. Their special day was a holiday for the whole kingdom.

But one man did not want them to live happily ever after.

There was a bad man named Haman who worked for King Xerxes. He hated the Israelites and made a plan to have all of them killed.

Esther's cousin Mordecai went very carefully to the palace and slipped a secret message to Esther. Mordecai's note said, "Haman wants to kill the Israelites. Help us!"

Mordecai told Esther, "Maybe God has made you the queen at this time so that you can protect God's people."

With her life in great danger, Esther went to the king with a special request. She decided that if she had to die, she would die serving God.

For two nights, Esther made special dinners for Haman and King Xerxes. After the meals, her husband said, "Esther, I'll give you anything you want, up to half my kingdom."

Aha! Esther thought. *It's time to tell my secret.* "Save me and my people," she said. "Your worker Haman is trying to kill us!"

"What?" the king shouted. He didn't care that Esther was an Israelite. When he learned that she might have been killed, he had Haman punished.

King Xerxes was kind to the Israelites, and to this day, Esther is remembered for protecting the lives of her people so that Jesus could be born through this family.

Jesus Calling

"For I know the plans I have for you,"
declares the LORD.

JEREMIAH 29:11

Even before you were born, I had a plan for your life.
You may not feel you are someone important.
But if you are willing,
I can use you in wonderful ways.
I have plans for you, and they are good.

Nehemiah the Builder | from Nehemiah 1–8

Crash! Bang! Bam! The enemy attacked Jerusalem, and its walls came tumbling down. When the Israelites in Persia heard about it, Nehemiah went to the king. "The enemy wrecked our city walls. We can't defend ourselves," he said. "Let me go home so I can rebuild the walls."

The king agreed. He made sure that Nehemiah got there safely and had everything he needed.

Nehemiah and his helpers went to work. And if anyone felt discouraged, Nehemiah cheered them on: "God is on our side! Come on. We can do it!"

Little by little, the walls went up, but the enemy was watching, so Nehemiah posted guards all around. He asked God to keep the workers safe and then kept on building no matter what. On went the stones. In went the heavy main gates. "Done!" Nehemiah shouted. Jerusalem was safe, and at last the Israelites could come home.

Jesus Calling

"Don't think that I have come to destroy the law of Moses or the teaching of the prophets. I have not come to destroy their teachings but to do what they said."

MATTHEW 5:17 ICB

Love God first, and love others as yourself.
This is the most important part of God's Law.
But the Israelites often followed the sins of the
countries around them instead of obeying the Law.
At times, the Israelites lost everything because they
didn't have faith in the One True God.
God used Nehemiah to bring some of them home
to Jerusalem, but they still needed a Savior.
God's people could never be good enough
to save themselves. So God sent Me, His Son—
the only One who could save His children forever.

THE NEW TESTAMENT

Finally, it was time. God was ready. The world was ready.
Stars sparkled in the sky on a night so quiet you could hear
your heart beat. If you stood still, closed your eyes,
and took a deep breath, you could feel something in the air.
The sky, the fields, and the little town of Bethlehem—
they were ready. The angels in heaven were ready.

This was the perfect time for Jesus to be born.

Mary Meets an Angel | from Luke 1

God's ways and timing are always perfect. The birth of His Son was no different. Before Jesus was born, God picked just the right parents for Jesus. His mom, Mary, was engaged to Joseph, the great-great-great-great-great- (and a lot more greats!) grandson of King David.

Mary was alone one day when an angel appeared right in front of her! She couldn't believe her eyes.

"Don't be afraid," said the gentle voice of God's angel Gabriel. "God is pleased with you. Soon you will have a baby boy. His name will be Jesus. This is the One the prophets spoke of. He will save God's people from their sins and rule the world forever."

Jesus, God's only Son, was coming down from heaven.

"How can this be true?" Mary asked. "I can't have a baby when I'm not married."

"God has a plan," Gabriel answered. "And there's more. Your cousin Elizabeth is having a baby too. Everyone thinks she is too old, but nothing is impossible for God."

Mary could not believe what she was hearing, but she trusted God. "I will do whatever God wants," she said. Then the angel disappeared as fast as he'd come.

A Baby Named John | from Luke 1

Elizabeth and her husband, Zechariah, were very old, and they had no children. One day Zechariah was in the temple worshiping God when the angel Gabriel appeared beside him. "Zechariah, soon you and Elizabeth will have a son. You must name him John. He will have important work to do for the Lord."

A baby? No way! Zechariah didn't believe the angel's words. "We are too old to be parents," he said in shock.

"Zechariah," Gabriel said, "because you do not believe, you won't be able to speak one word until he is born." Then Gabriel disappeared, and Zechariah was . . . well . . . speechless!

Sure enough, Elizabeth had a baby boy. Zechariah and Elizabeth praised God and wondered about His plan for their little boy.

"What will you name him?" someone asked. Zechariah wrote on a tablet, *His name is John.*

Suddenly, he felt words tumble from his mouth, "His name is John!" From then on, Zechariah could speak again.

Jesus Calling

"The time has come," [Jesus] said.
"The kingdom of God is near.
Repent and believe the good news!"

MARK 1:15

When the time was just right, God sent angels to announce My birth and the birth of My cousin John the Baptist. God sent John to be a messenger who told people to repent and get ready for Me. My Father in heaven sent Me to save you from your sins. This is *very* good news!

He's Here! | from Luke 2; Matthew 1–2

The emperor wanted to know how many people lived on his land, so he had everyone go to their hometowns to be counted. It was nighttime when Joseph and Mary arrived in Bethlehem. The little town was crammed with people. Every room was taken, and the only place left to rest was a stable filled with sleepy animals. There, Joseph made a bed for Mary in the hay. Little did the world know that the most awesome, amazing, and almighty part of God's plan was beginning. Jesus was ready to be born.

In the stillness of the night He came—God's gift of Christmas—
the One who would save the world. Joseph named Him Jesus.
As the cows, horses, goats, and sheep watched, Mary wrapped
her baby in soft cloths to keep Him warm. Then she laid Him
in hay in the animals' feeding trough.

God gave the world hope through a tiny baby lying in a manger.

145

In the fields near Bethlehem, shepherds were guarding their sheep. Suddenly, a scary bright light flashed in the sky. And many, many angels appeared, singing praises to God.

A glowing angel said, "Don't be afraid! I have good news for you, which will make everyone happy. This very day in King David's hometown a Savior was born for you. He is Christ the Lord. You will know who he is, because you will find Him dressed in baby cloths and lying on a bed of hay" (Luke 2:10–12 CEV).

"Wow! That's amazing!" the shepherds exclaimed to each other as they hurried off to Bethlehem to find Jesus. They were excited to see the Son of God, and they knelt down and worshiped Jesus as soon as they found Him. Then they went out and spread the word about what the angel had told them. And Mary? She spent the night wide awake, thanking God and thinking about His mysterious, wonderful plan.

Jesus Calling

But I trust in your unfailing love;
my heart rejoices in your salvation.

PSALM 13:5

On that special night so many years ago,
people rejoiced at My coming into their world.
Even though you cannot see or touch Me,
I am still very present in your world today.
I am right here beside you. I have always loved you.
Even before the creation of the world,
I chose you to be My child.

In the Far East, some wise men saw a bright star in the sky.
"It's His star!" one of them said. "A sign from God." So they set
out on a very long journey, following the star, searching for
the little King of kings.

They stopped in Jerusalem, where King Herod ruled, and asked
for directions. Herod was an evil king. He felt jealous to hear
of this baby King, Jesus. *No one is more of a king than I am*,
Herod complained to himself.

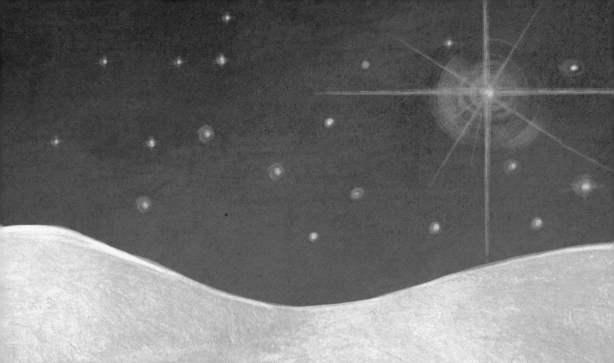

King Herod lied to the wise men, "When you find Jesus, come back and tell me exactly where He is. I want to go worship Him too."

Then the wise men followed the star to Bethlehem. And there they found Jesus and Mary. They knelt down and worshiped Jesus and gave Him gifts fit for a king. But God warned them in a dream not to tell Herod where to find Jesus. The wise men obeyed God and went home by another road.

When King Herod heard that the wise men had tricked him, oh boy, was he mad! He became so jealous of Jesus that he ordered his men to kill all the boys two years old and under in Bethlehem and the surrounding area. Well, God wasn't going to let that happen to the world's Savior. He sent an angel to warn Joseph: "Hurry! Take Mary and Jesus to Egypt. Stay there until I tell you to come back, because Herod wants to kill God's Son."

In the darkness of night, when no one saw, Joseph slipped away to Egypt with Mary and Jesus. They stayed there safely until the evil King Herod died.

Jesus Calling

You know that our Lord Jesus Christ was kind enough to give up all his riches and become poor, so that you could become rich.

2 CORINTHIANS 8:9 CEV

I left the comfort of My heavenly home to be born in a dirty stable. I gave up all of My heavenly riches and became poor so that you could become rich. When you trust Me as your Savior, I give you the best riches of all— better than all the gold in the world! I give you Life that will go on forever and ever.

Jesus the Boy | from Luke 2

When Jesus was a boy, His family traveled to Jerusalem for the Passover celebration. On the way home, the crowd was so huge that Jesus' parents lost track of Him. They thought He was walking with friends, but He wasn't. It took a whole day before they discovered that Jesus was missing.

They hurried back to Jerusalem, asking all the way, "Has anyone seen our boy?" Finally, they found Jesus in the temple, listening to the teachers and asking questions. The teachers were amazed by how much Jesus knew about God's truths.

"Where have You been?" His parents scolded. "We've been looking for You."

"Didn't you know that I would be in my Father's house?" Jesus answered. Jesus was telling His parents that although He loved and obeyed them, He knew that He was the Son of God the Father.

Jesus Calling

I deeply love your Law! I think about it all day.

PSALM 119:97 CEV

Listen to My words in the Bible.
Ask questions so that you understand.
Think about all the things I taught, and think about
Me. As you learn more and spend time
talking with Me, you become more like Me.
This makes Me happy,
and it will make you happy too.

John the Baptist | from Matthew 3

Jesus' cousin, John, grew into a big, strong man. He lived outdoors, wore camel-hair clothes, and ate locusts (which are like crispy grasshoppers) covered with honey. John's job was to get people ready for Jesus. "The Savior is coming!" he shouted. "Prepare for Him! Ask forgiveness for the things you have done wrong!"

Crowds of people followed John, and he baptized each person in the river. Their baptism showed God (and everyone who was watching) that they loved God and were sorry for their sins.

One day, John saw Jesus standing in the crowd, waiting to be baptized. *Oh my*, he thought, *Jesus is the Son of God. He is the One to forgive people of their sins. I can't baptize the Savior.*

"I should be baptized by You!" he said to Jesus.

But Jesus answered, "This is what God the Father wants us to do." So John baptized Him. Then the sky opened up, and the Holy Spirit came down from heaven like a dove, and God the Father said, "This is My dear Son, and I am very pleased with Him."

Jesus Calling

God was pleased for all of himself to live in Christ. And through Christ, God has brought all things back to himself again—things on earth and things in heaven. God made peace through the blood of Christ's death on the cross.

COLOSSIANS 1:19–20 NCV

When I came to live on the earth, God the Father was very pleased with Me. He was glad I was sharing His love with people so they could come to Him through Me. When you open your heart to Me and let My love shine through you to others, I am very pleased with *you*.

Twelve Helpers
from Matthew 4; 10; Luke 5

Jesus had the best news ever! He knew the biggest and best part of God's plan, which was to save people from their sins so that they could live forever with Him in heaven. Jesus wanted helpers to spread the news and tell everyone in the world about what God was doing.

Did He look for helpers who were really smart? No. Did He look for rich people who could use their money to help? No. Jesus looked for ordinary sinful people who did ordinary things.

Jesus went walking near the Sea of Galilee. There He saw two fishermen casting their nets. The men were brothers, Peter and Andrew.

"Come, follow Me," Jesus called to them. "I will make you fishers of men." Peter and Andrew knew in their hearts that Jesus was God's Son, so they left their work behind to join Him. Then Jesus saw two more brothers, James and John, fixing nets in a boat with their dad. "Come, follow Me!" He said again. They also left their jobs as fishermen to go with Jesus and be His helpers. Instead of catching fish, they would go and "catch" people so they could know Jesus too!

Jesus gathered more helpers—called *disciples*—along the way:
Philip, Bartholomew, Thomas, Thaddaeus, another young man named
James, Simon, Judas, and a tax collector named Matthew.

Matthew hung out with sinners, but that didn't bother Jesus.
He already knew that Matthew would leave everything behind—
his money and his job—to be a helper.

"Will you follow Me?" Jesus asked Matthew.

"I will!" Matthew said. "Yes, I will!" Matthew was so happy that he invited his friends to dinner so they could meet Jesus and the other disciples. But some wondered why Jesus would eat with a bunch of sinners. "I came to save them," Jesus said. "They need Me most of all."

Jesus didn't run from sinners. More than anything, He wanted them to be rescued. Jesus and His helpers—the twelve disciples—wanted everyone to know about God's great plan.

Jesus Calling

"Follow Me, and I will make you fishers of men."
MATTHEW 4:19 NKJV

You don't have to be perfect to follow Me.
You only need to believe in Me and trust Me
as your Savior. *You* can be one of My helpers too.
Tell your family and friends the good news
that I came to save the world from sin.
Tell them that if they believe in Me, they can
one day live forever with Me in heaven!

Jesus the Teacher
The Beatitudes | from Matthew 5

Jesus had amazing things to say, and wherever He and His helpers went, big crowds followed. One day, Jesus told the people about God's blessings.

Jesus taught about eight important blessings. The Bible has a special name for them—the Beatitudes.

"These people will be very blessed," Jesus said, "and here is how they will be blessed":

*Those who believe they are sinful will be part of God's family.
Those who are sad for their sins will be comforted by God.
Those who are humble and obey God will inherit the new earth.
Those who desire to do what is right will know they have
    God's righteousness.
Those who are kind and forgiving toward others will receive
    forgiveness from God.
Those whose hearts are forgiven will see God as He is in heaven.
Those who help others find peace with God are peacemakers,
    and God calls them His children.
Those who tell others about God, even when people hurt them,
    are part of God's family.*

Jesus the Teacher
The Lord's Prayer | from Matthew 6

Jesus also taught the people a special prayer called the Lord's Prayer.

> *"Our Father in heaven,*
> *help us to honor your name.*
> *Come and set up your kingdom,*
> *so that everyone on earth will obey you,*
> *as you are obeyed in heaven.*
>
> *Give us our food for today.*
> *Forgive us for doing wrong,*
> *as we forgive others.*
>
> *Keep us from being tempted*
> *and protect us from evil.*
> *The kingdom, the power,*
> *and the glory are yours forever. Amen."* CEV

Jesus said, "When you pray, go to your room, shut the door, and talk with God the Father. He will hear you every time."

Do Not Worry | from Matthew 6

Jesus knows it's easy for people to worry about things, but He wants everyone to know that He can be trusted to take care of us. He told the people in His day, "Look at the birds in the sky. They don't have to grow or buy their food, but God takes care of them. And look at the beautiful flowers! Even the great King Solomon wasn't covered in such beauty. How much more will your heavenly Father take care of you? God knows you need these things, and when you seek Him first in your life, all of these needs will be taken care of."

He says the same thing to us in the Bible today.

Jesus the Teacher
The Greatest Commandment | from Matthew 7: 22

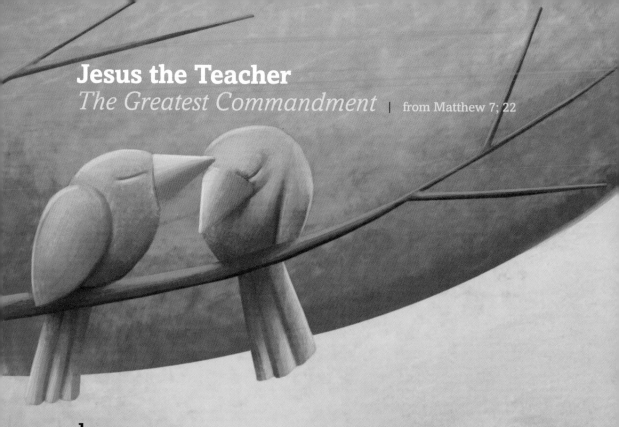

Jesus had advice for bullies (and for people who are sometimes bullied): "Treat others as you want them to treat you." This verse is called the Golden Rule.

Jesus said the greatest commandment is to love God with all our hearts, souls, and minds. And the second greatest commandment is to love our neighbors as ourselves. When we love God and other people this way, we will be kind to them, even if they aren't kind to us!

Jesus Calling

"Treat others the same way you want them to treat you."

LUKE 6:31 NASB

When others treat you unfairly, think about
how I treat you. I don't say mean things to you.
I offer to help you, and I bless you with My Love.
This is how I want you to be toward others.
So try to be loving with others—brothers, sisters,
mom, dad, friends, teachers. This pleases Me.

Jesus' Great Stories
The Farmer and His Seeds | from Matthew 13

Jesus told wonderful stories, called *parables*, to help people understand God's kingdom and know that Jesus is the King. He told them important truths through simple stories about things in their everyday lives:

"A farmer went to plant seeds. Some seeds fell on a road, and the birds came and gobbled them up. Some sprouted in rocky soil but died because their roots weren't deep enough to find water. Others fell among weeds. When they sprouted, the weeds choked them. But a few seeds fell on good ground, and they grew tall and strong. At harvest time, the farmer said, 'Oh my! Those few seeds have produced bushels and bushels of grain, a hundred times as much as was planted.'"

Jesus explained His story. "I am like a farmer planting God's words in different places. The seeds are like people. People on the road hear My Father's words, but they don't understand them. Then Satan comes like the birds and snatches those precious words away. People on rocky soil accept God's words for a while and then give up. They aren't strong enough to keep growing. Those in the weeds are too busy with wants and worries to understand God's words. But the people on good ground hear and believe. Because I love them, they are very thankful, and they show Me by loving others."

Jesus' Great Stories

The Little Lost Lamb | from Luke 15

Jesus once told a story about a cute little lamb that lived in a pasture with ninety-nine other sheep. The shepherd took very good care of his sheep. He fed them, gave them water, and chased away wild animals. But one day, the shepherd noticed his lamb was missing. Right away, he left the other ninety-nine and went looking. When he found the lamb, he shouted, "Hurray!"

God the Father is like that shepherd. He doesn't want any of His children to be lost. He wants all His children to stay close to Him. And just as a good shepherd leads his sheep home, God will lead to heaven everyone who says they are sorry for their sins and believes in Jesus.

The Treasure | from Matthew 13

Jesus also told a story about the world's greatest treasure. He said, "A man found a treasure hidden in a field. When he found it, he hid it again. Then he sold everything he had and bought that field."

Jesus is the treasure. Once you find Him, you want to believe in Jesus and make sure He is more important than anything else in your life. The man in Jesus' story sold everything he had and bought the field so he could hold on to his treasure forever.

Jesus' Great Stories
The Lost Coin | from Luke 15

Jesus also told a story about a woman who had ten silver coins but lost one in her house. She needed some light to see where it was, so she lit a lamp. She still couldn't find her coin, so she swept the whole house. Now she had a very clean house but no coin. She looked up and down, back and forth, inside, outside, around, and through, and finally . . .

She found it! She called her friends and neighbors and said, "Let's have a party! I've found my lost coin!"

What does Jesus' parable mean? When one sinful person says, "I'm sorry," to God and wants to change for good, then all of heaven's angels celebrate. Heaven has big parties all the time for sinners who have been forgiven!

Jesus Calling

We must keep our eyes on Jesus,
who leads us and makes our faith complete.

HEBREWS 12:2 CEV

Try to keep thinking about Me—even when you're doing other things. I don't want you to get separated from Me like the little lamb. But if you do, I will come for you and bring you back to where you belong. I tell these stories so you will understand how important you are to Me. You are so precious that I gave up everything— even My life—to find you and keep you close to Me.

Jesus' Great Stories
The Prodigal Son | from Luke 15

Once, there were two brothers, and the younger one was unhappy. We don't know why. Maybe he was bored. Maybe he didn't like where he lived. Whatever the reason, he decided to leave home. He went to his dad and said, "Give me my share of the money I would get after you die—only I want it *now*." This was a very selfish request.

The young man set out to see the world. He went wherever he wanted and did whatever he wanted, including lots of things he shouldn't have done. He made very bad friends and spent all his money. Soon he didn't have enough to buy food. His tummy growled. So he went to work for a man in the country— feeding his pigs. He worked hard, but the pig farmer didn't give him anything to eat. When the icky, sloppy piggy food started looking like a feast, the young man decided that home wasn't so bad after all.

The son headed for home, knowing that he had treated God and his father badly. But as soon as his dad saw him coming, the old man ran to meet his son, hugging and kissing him.

"Dad," the young man said, "I'm really, really sorry."

What did his dad do? He forgave the son. Then the father threw a big "Welcome Home!" party. He served his best food, and everyone sang and danced. But boy, did the older brother get mad!

"Dad!" he cried. "I've been good and always obeyed you, and you never threw a big party for me."

"My dear son," his dad said, "you are with me all the time, and all I have is yours. Today we need to celebrate, because your brother has been lost, and now he is found."

And it's like that with God. He and the angels celebrate when someone repents. God wants all His children to be happy and rejoice when sinful people change their ways and believe in Jesus as their Savior.

Jesus Calling

"Love the LORD your God with all your heart, with all your soul, and with all your mind."

MATTHEW 22:37 NKJV

Many things cause your mind to wander from Me: a game, your homework, playing with your friends. When your mind gets too far away from Me, My Spirit will whisper to you gently, reminding you to return to Me. Don't ignore those whispers. You are always going to be happiest when your heart is close to Mine.

Jesus' Great Stories

The Good Samaritan   from Luke 10

Some people didn't like Jesus, so they tried to trick Him with questions. "God's Law says, 'Love your neighbors as much as you love yourself.' So, who is my neighbor?" they asked.

Jesus answered with a story:

"A man walked alone on a country road. Robbers attacked him; they beat him and stole everything he had. A teacher of God's Law saw the man lying in the road, but he passed by without helping. Another religious man came along, but he looked the other way too.

"Finally, a man from Samaria came along. He saw the injured man lying there, and he hurried to help. He bandaged his wounds and took him to the nearest inn and cared for him. With his own money, he provided for the man until he was well. Which of these three people was the best neighbor?"

Jesus knew that the wise teachers didn't like people from Samaria, but now they had to admit that the Samaritan had done what was right.

"The one who helped," they answered.

"That's right," Jesus said. "And that's what you should do." Anyone and everyone is our neighbor.

Jesus Calling

If you really keep the royal law found in Scripture, "Love your neighbor as yourself," you are doing right.

JAMES 2:8

I want you to show love and kindness
to those who are different from you,
and even to those who are mean to you.
This shows everyone your great love for Me!
Ask Me to help you love other people with *My* Love.
Let it flow through you to others.

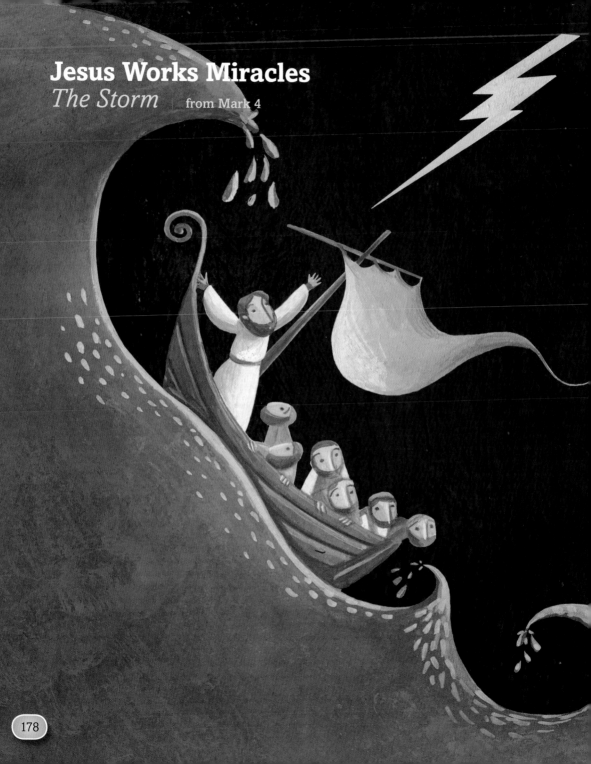

Jesus Works Miracles
The Storm   from Mark 4

All day long, Jesus taught big crowds of people about God. Jesus was very tired. So when evening came, He said to His disciples, "Let's go in our boat to the other side of the lake." While they were sailing, Jesus fell asleep. Some of His disciples were fishermen; they knew everything about sailing and steering a boat. Surely they didn't need Jesus' help. But then a huge thunderstorm came up. Thunder—*BOOM!* Lightning—*FLASH!* A big wind came whistling and howling and racing across the water, right at them. By this time, they were in the middle of the lake, and there was nothing they could do.

The small boat rocked from side to side. And as it rocked, water poured in. "We're going to sink!" cried one of the men. Even the fishermen who knew all about sailing were terrified. "Wake up, Jesus!" they shouted. "Save us!"

Jesus stood up, and He said to the wind, "Stop." And it stopped.

"Why were you so afraid?" He asked His disciples. "Don't you have any faith?"

"Who is this?" the disciples whispered to each other. "Even the wind obeys Him."

Jesus is God's Son, and He is greater than wind, waves, and our biggest fears.

Jesus Works Miracles
The Fishes and Loaves | from John 6

People heard about the many miracles Jesus did—giving sight to the blind, calming storms, and healing the sick. Five thousand men, plus women and children, came to a hillside to hear Jesus teach one day. He talked to them for hours and hours, telling them about His Father, God in heaven.

It was nearly dinnertime, and the disciples had nothing to feed the crowd. So James whispered to Jesus, "Send them home now. The people are getting hungry." But Jesus said, "Find something for them to eat."

What? It would take eight months' salary to feed this many people! They didn't have any food and certainly didn't have that kind of money. But the disciples looked around to see what they could find, and they spied a little boy carrying a picnic basket with five small loaves of bread and two little fish. Jesus took the loaves and fishes, gave thanks to God the Father, and had the disciples pass out the food. There was enough bread and fish to feed everyone as much as they wanted.

"Gather up all the leftovers. We don't want to waste anything," Jesus said. There were twelve baskets with leftover fish and bread. In this way, Jesus was able to show His endless love for hungry people.

The people were amazed! "Surely, this man is from God," they said.

Jesus Calling

I pray that God will take care of all your needs with the wonderful blessings that come from Christ Jesus!

PHILIPPIANS 4:19 CEV

I did not create you to do things on your own. I made you to need Me—not only for things like your food, clothes, and home. You also need Me to fill you up inside with a goodness that only I can bring. Come to Me and ask for everything you need. Trust Me to fill you with My goodness and to take wonderful care of you.

Jesus Works Miracles
Jesus Walks on Water | from Matthew 14

After everyone ate that miraculous meal and it was time to go, Jesus told the disciples to sail their boat to the other side of the lake. Jesus stayed behind to pray.

The boat was far from shore when a big storm came up. The wind and waves rocked the little boat to the left, then to the right. As the men fought to keep from sinking, they saw something—someone—walking toward them on the water. Yikes! Their bodies shook with fear. They screamed, "A ghost! A ghost!"

The figure came closer. Then the men saw that it wasn't a ghost, but Jesus. "Don't be afraid," Jesus said.

Peter said, "Lord, if it's really You, tell me to walk to You on the water."

So Jesus said, "Come."

Brave Peter climbed out of the boat, and he started walking on the water toward Jesus. But as soon as he thought about what he was doing—really walking on top of the water—Peter got scared. Down he went into the sea, yelling, "Save me, Lord!"

Jesus grabbed Peter's hand. "Why did you lose faith?" Jesus asked as He pulled Peter, all soggy and squishy, into the boat.

Now the men believed: This really was Jesus, the Son of God.

Jesus Calling

*Everyone who calls on the name
of the Lord will be saved.*

ACTS 2:21

All people need saving because they are drowning in sin. Just as I was there for Peter, I am there for everyone who calls on Me. I know it is sometimes hard to trust Me. Remember that I am the Son of God, and when you call on Me, I will save you. As you ask Me to forgive your sins and you pray, "Lord, save me!" I will be there immediately. I will reach for you and keep you safe.

Mary and Martha | from Luke 10

When Jesus needed a rest, He spent time visiting His friends. Some of His very best friends were a man named Lazarus and his sisters, Mary and Martha.

Jesus showed up at Martha's house one day while Mary was there. Both women were happy to see Him, but Martha said, "Oh, dear. Please excuse the way my house looks. It's a mess." She told Jesus to sit down and relax, and then she got busy trying to make things perfect.

Martha dusted and swept and began cooking a special dinner for Jesus. Meanwhile, Mary sat at Jesus' feet, listening to everything He said. *Why is Mary just sitting around?* Martha wondered. Martha grumbled to Jesus, "Don't You care that Mary has let me do all the work? Tell her to help me!"

"Martha," Jesus said, "Mary has chosen what is right, and I won't take it away from her."

Mary chose to put Jesus first. She knew that spending time with Him was much more important than anything else she could do.

Jesus Calling

"Come to me, all you who are weary and burdened, and I will give you rest."

MATTHEW 11:28

Every day, there are many things you could do.
Some are good; some are important. But none
are as good or important as being with Me.
Spend time talking with Me and reading
Bible stories. It's the best thing you will ever do.
It will put Joy in your heart that is so big and
so bright, it will shine for all to see.

Jesus Heals the Sick
Jairus's Daughter and the Sick Woman

| from Mark 5

A big crowd had gathered around Jesus. Pushing through all the people, an important man named Jairus knelt at Jesus' feet and begged, "My little girl is dying. Please come home with me and make her well again."

"Let's go," Jesus said. The crowd followed, shoving and hurrying toward Jairus's house to see what Jesus would do.

In the crowd was a woman who had been sick for twelve years.
None of the doctors could fix her, but she believed that Jesus would.
If I can just touch Him, I will get well, she thought. She reached
through the crowd toward Jesus. Then, with just her fingertips,
she touched the edge of His robe.

"Who touched Me?" Jesus asked, stopping and turning around.
How could He have felt that soft touch with all those people pressing
around Him? The woman looked embarrassed but came forward.
Jesus smiled and spoke kindly to her, "Your faith has made you well.
You will be free from this suffering."

"Jairus! Jairus!" A man came running up to him. "Your daughter has died."

But Jesus said to Jairus, "Don't worry. Just have faith. Follow Me."

At Jairus's house, people stood crying at the bedside of the little girl who lay so still. "Why are you crying?" Jesus asked. "She's not dead. She's sleeping."

Was Jesus crazy? Jairus's friends and family thought so. They even laughed at Him, but that didn't stop Jesus. He sent everyone out except for Jairus and his wife and the three disciples who'd come with him, Peter, James, and John.

Jesus went to the little girl and gently picked up her lifeless hand. He held it in His, and in a sweet voice, He said, "Little girl. Get up!" She opened her eyes and smiled at Him. Then she stood and walked around as if she had never been sick—and died!

Her parents wanted to tell everyone what Jesus had done, but Jesus ordered them not to.

Jesus Calling

"Do not be afraid; only believe."

MARK 5:36 NKJV

No matter what is happening, you can always know that I have a plan for you and that I am with you. So trust Me, and don't be afraid—even when you have big problems in your life. No problem is too big for Me!

Jesus Heals the Sick
The Blind Man | from John 9

Jesus did miracles for two reasons—to show His love for people and to prove that He is God and has all power to heal and to give eternal life to those who believe in Him.

A blind man sat begging on the roadside. "A penny for a poor man?" he called out to people passing by.

"Teacher," one of the disciples asked as they came near, "is this man blind because he has sinned?"

"No," Jesus answered. "He was born blind so he and others will know what God can do."

Then Jesus did something rather strange. He stopped, spit on the ground, and made mud with His spit. He rubbed it on the man's eyes and said, "Now, go. Wash it off."

The man went and washed. When the mud was cleared from his eyes, he shouted, "I can see!" He ran home so happy. People had many questions, but the man simply said, "I don't have all the answers. The one thing I know for sure is this: I once was blind, but now I see!"

Jesus Calling

[Jesus] said, "I am the light of the world. Whoever follows me will never walk in darkness, but will have the light of life."

JOHN 8:12

The blind man lived in darkness until I healed his eyes. Many people live in a different kind of darkness because they don't know Me as their Savior. When you open your heart to Me, I fill you with the Light of Life. This gift of Life will last forever and ever.

Jesus Heals the Sick

Ten Lepers | from Luke 17

In Jesus' day, people sometimes got so excited about being healed that they forgot to thank Him. Like the nine lepers. Leprosy is a terrible disease that makes awful sores all over a person's body. It was easily passed to others, so lepers had to live away from their friends and families. Ten lepers heard that Jesus was coming to a nearby village, and they hoped that maybe, just maybe, He might heal them. They hid near the road and waited.

When they saw Him, they shouted, "Master, have pity on us!" Jesus looked at them and said, "Go to the priests." What did that mean? If a leper got healed, he had to prove to a priest that he was well again. But these lepers were still sick! Off to the priests they went anyway, and on the way there—*bam!*—they were healed!

They hurried off to tell their friends. But only one man came back. He fell at Jesus' feet and cried, "Thank You, Jesus! Thank You, and praise be to God!"

"Where are the other nine?" Jesus asked. Only the one man came back to thank Jesus.

Jesus Calling

Give thanks to the LORD, for he is good.
His love endures forever.

PSALM 136:1

I love hearing you thank Me. Try to count all the blessings I give you. A thankful heart will keep you close to Me.

Jesus Heals the Sick

Lazarus Is Raised! | from John 11

One day Mary and Martha's brother, Lazarus, got very sick. His sisters sent for Jesus, who was teaching in another village, but Jesus did not come to their house for two days.

When Jesus arrived, Lazarus had already died. His sisters were very upset. "Where were You? We thought You loved Lazarus. If You had been here, You could have healed him." They cried, and Jesus cried too.

"Have faith," He told them. "Believe in Me."

The villagers gathered around Lazarus's tomb. "Open it up," Jesus said.

"He died four days ago," Martha argued. "The smell will be terrible."

"Open it," Jesus said. Then He prayed, "Thank You, Father, for answering My prayer. I know You answer prayer, but I want these people to believe that You sent Me."

Next He shouted, "Lazarus, come out!" Slowly, Lazarus stumbled out of the grave, wrapped in linen like a mummy.

"He's alive!" the people gasped. "This man Jesus really is the Son of God."

Jesus Calling

Jesus then said, "I am the one who raises the dead to life! Everyone who has faith in me will live, even if they die."

JOHN 11:25 CEV

I am God's Holy Son, and I came to earth to save God's people. Everyone has a body that will someday die. But if you believe in Me as your Savior, you will live again. You will live with Me forever in heaven!

Zacchaeus Meets Jesus | from Luke 19

So many people wanted to meet Jesus! After all, He healed diseases, gave blind men sight, and brought dead people to life. Zacchaeus wanted to meet Jesus too, but he was a little guy who couldn't see over the heads of the crowds. He couldn't count on anyone to lift him up either, because Zacchaeus had no friends. He worked as a tax collector, and no one liked tax collectors. They often took people's money unfairly.

If Zacchaeus was going to see Jesus, he would have to climb a tree.

Jesus knew that Zacchaeus had no friends. He knew that Zacchaeus was up in that tree. Stopping underneath the tree, He looked up and said, "Come down, Zacchaeus. I'm staying at your house today."

What? My house? Zacchaeus thought. Meanwhile, everyone grumbled, "Why is Jesus going to his house? That little man is a sinner if ever there was one!"

Zacchaeus didn't often obey God; he was lost in sin. Yet later, at the house, Zacchaeus told Jesus he was sorry for cheating people and promised that he would make it up to them by returning the money he had stolen.

"Wonderful!" Jesus said. "Now, instead of being punished by God, you will live with Me in heaven."

Zacchaeus was no longer a cheat! And finally, Zacchaeus had a friend, the best Friend of all—Jesus.

Jesus Calling

Jesus said, "It is not the healthy who need a doctor, but the sick."
MATTHEW 9:12

When I was on the earth, people often got angry because I spent so much time with sinners. But *all* people are "sick" with sin, even if they think they are healthy. And I'm the only doctor who can heal the sickness of sin. Instead of pointing at other people's sin, tell them about Me. I'm the sin-doctor who can heal them—and you.

Jesus Loves You! | from Mark 10

The kids in the place that Jesus was visiting wanted to see Him: little kids, big kids, girl kids, boy kids, kids of every size and color. Moms and dads wanted Jesus to bless their children and pray for them. But Jesus' disciples said, "No, don't bother the Teacher. Take the children away."

Jesus didn't like that. "Let the children come to Me," He said. "Don't try to stop them." So all the kids hurried over to Jesus. They hugged Him. Some sat on His lap. They asked Him questions, laughed together—and Jesus loved every minute of it.

Jesus said a really nice thing about children: He said that they know best how to trust God. If grownups trusted God the way kids do, it would be easier for them to know how to go to heaven.

Before the children left Jesus that day, He blessed them and gave each one a great big hug.

Jesus loves kids, and He loves you!

Jesus Calling

"Let the little children come to Me."

MARK 10:14 NKJV

Oh, how I love to hear My children laugh! I want you to come to Me, no matter how you are feeling— when you are happy and can't stop smiling, when you are sad and want to cry, when you are mad, and even when you are ashamed or embarrassed. I understand everything about you— including all your feelings. And I love you.

The Widow's Gift | from Mark 12

"Watch out for them!" Jesus told His disciples. He was talking about a group of religious show-offs who acted better than everyone else. They wore expensive robes and prayed loudly in the marketplace, "O God, look at us. See how good we are?" They thought they were special because of their religion and what their money could buy. Yet they thought nothing about true faith and didn't really care about helping the poor.

Jesus knew how they would end up. "God will punish them," He said.

Jesus and His disciples were in the temple, watching people drop money into the collection box. Many rich people gave a lot. But then a poor woman, whose husband had died, quietly dropped in two coins. "Look," Jesus said. "She had nothing left but those two coins, worth only a few pennies. Others gave what they didn't need. She gave everything she had. She gave more than all the others."

God doesn't want us to show off about what we can do for Him. He wants us to quietly serve Him—with all our hearts and with all we have to give.

Jesus Calling

*I will praise God's name in song
and glorify him with thanksgiving.*

PSALM 69:30

If I have given you the ability to do something well, remember to thank Me for that gift. Be careful not to be a show-off when you use your gift. Instead, use your abilities—the things you're really good at—to glorify *Me*. When you do your very best with a thankful heart because you are My child, you bring Me Glory!

The Glory of Jesus | from Matthew 17; Mark 9; Luke 9

Peter, James, and John were Jesus' closest friends. One day, Jesus took them up on a mountain with Him to pray. The disciples had seen a lot of amazing miracles, but nothing could have prepared them for what they were about to see next.

While Jesus was praying, a brilliant light surrounded Him. His face was changed, and His robe was glistening white. Suddenly Elijah and Moses appeared and were talking with Jesus. The three disciples were stunned as they watched, for Elijah and Moses had been dead for hundreds of years!

Then a cloud covered them, and the voice of God the Father boomed from heaven, "This is my beloved Son. Listen to Him!" The disciples fell on their faces before God. Then, just as suddenly as it all happened, the cloud disappeared, and so did Elijah and Moses.

When Peter, James, and John looked up, Jesus was still with them. As they came down the mountain, Jesus told them, "One day I will rise from the dead, but first I will have to suffer a lot. Until then, don't tell anyone what you have just seen."

Jesus Calling

[God said,] "This is my Son, whom I love. Listen to him!"

MARK 9:7

Listen to My words with your heart.
During the day I will whisper words of love to you;
at night I will sing you a lullaby of peace. Also,
read about Me in the Bible, and learn all
the wonderful things I am teaching you.

Palm Sunday | from Matthew 21; John 12

Something terrible yet wonderful was about to happen. In a few days, God's big plan would be revealed. Jesus knew what was coming, and God knew. But no one else did.

On the way to Jerusalem, Jesus sent two disciples ahead to find a donkey for Him to ride into the city. Jesus climbed onto its back and, *clippity-clop*, He rode it through the open city gates.

Jerusalem was filled with families preparing for Passover, the year's biggest holiday. "Look! It's Jesus!" someone shouted. They all ran to see Him. Some laid their coats on the dirty road for the donkey to walk on. Others covered the street with palm branches or waved them in the air. "Hosanna! Hurray! The Son of David is here!" they yelled. "Blessed is Jesus, who comes in the name of the Lord!"

Jesus rode into the city like a king, and Jerusalem's religious leaders didn't like that one bit. "Why are the people saying He comes in the name of the Lord?" they grumbled. "There's no way He can be the Son of God."

They were so angry that they made a plan to kill Jesus.

Jesus Calling

"In this world you will have trouble. But take heart!
I have overcome the world."

JOHN 16:33

There are times when people are nice to you,
and then later, they are mean.
When people hurt you, remember that I am with
you. I know how much it hurts, because they treated
Me that way too. Just stay close to Me.
I will help you get through your hard times.
And I will comfort you with My Peace.

The Last Supper

from Matthew 26; Mark 14; Luke 22; John 13

Jesus and His disciples gathered in an upstairs room to eat their Passover supper. During the meal, Jesus washed His disciples' feet. In those days, people's feet got very dirty walking in sandals on those dusty roads. Who would want to wash someone else's stinky feet?

Servants were the ones who had to wash people's feet back then. But Jesus served His disciples by doing this dirty job. At first, Peter didn't want Jesus to wash his feet

"Lord!" Peter said. "You are too good to wash my feet like a servant."

"But if you don't let Me wash away the dirt," Jesus answered, "you won't belong to Me."

Jesus wasn't talking about dirty feet, but about sin—the dirt in our hearts. When our hearts are full of things God hates, we can't be close to Him. It's impossible for people to wash away sin by themselves, and God knew that. So He planned for Jesus to wash our sins away, not by washing our feet but by washing our hearts.

After Jesus washed His disciples' feet, He said to them, "I did this to show you that as future servants and teachers, you are to be humble and do anything God asks, out of love for Me."

Jesus knew this was His last supper with His friends. "Soon I will leave you," He said. He picked up some bread, broke it into pieces, and passed it around for them to eat. "My body will be broken like this bread." He passed around a cup and told them to drink. "My blood will wash away your sins, and your hearts will be clean forever. Whenever you eat and drink, remember Me. I came to save God's people.

"One of you will have me arrested," Jesus said. The disciples couldn't believe what they were hearing. "*Who* would do this?" they asked. "The one to whom I will give this bread," Jesus said as he handed the bread to Judas. "Go. Do what you must."

Then Jesus said to the rest of His helpers, "I won't be with you much longer. You will be sad, but don't be afraid. I will come back."

Peter cried out, "I won't leave You. I'll be arrested and die with You!"

"Peter," Jesus said gently, "before the rooster crows tomorrow, you will say that you don't know Me three different times."

Jesus Calling

If you suffer as a Christian, do not be ashamed,
but praise God that you bear that name.

1 PETER 4:16

Sometimes it will be hard to tell others that you know Me. People may make fun of you and say bad things about you. But when you are treated that way for being a Christian, praise Me. You will be storing up treasures for yourself in heaven—treasures that are worth so much more than anything in this world!

Jesus Is Arrested | from Matthew 26; Mark 14; Luke 22; John 18

Jesus and His three closest friends—Peter, James, and John—
went outside after supper to a Garden near some olive trees.
Stars shone brightly in the sky, and the air smelled sweet.
Only He knew that soon the world would change forever.

"Wait here," Jesus told His disciples. He went alone into the
Garden to pray. "Father, please," He said. "Isn't there another
way without so much suffering? I don't want to be separated
from You. But Father, I will do whatever You want."

210

There was no other way. Jesus knew that God would have to lay all the sins of His children on Jesus' shoulders to save them from their punishment. And for those hours while Jesus suffered, He would be separated from the Father He loved because sin has no place with God. That would be the worst. But Jesus would do it to save men and women, boys and girls from God's judgment.

Then He heard the clanking of the soldiers' swords and smelled their torches burning. They pushed into the Garden with Judas leading them. Judas showed the guards which man was Jesus.

Jesus Calling

"There is no greater love than this—that a man should lay down his life for his friends."

JOHN 15:13 PHILLIPS

I love you with a Love that never ends. I loved you before you were born, and I will continue to love you forever. On that dark night so long ago, I allowed Myself to be killed on a cross because of My unstoppable Love for you. Whenever you feel alone or afraid, say it out loud: "Jesus, You are always with me, and You will never stop loving me."

Peter Denies Jesus | from Luke 22

Soldiers dragged Jesus through the streets to Jerusalem's leaders. "Are you the Son of God?" they asked.

"I am," Jesus said.

"Liar!" they shouted. "How dare you disrespect God by saying you're His Son!"

Soldiers whipped Him. Beat Him. Spit on Him. They made Him wear a purple robe and a crown of sharp thorns. And they made fun of Him. "Now You look like the King of the Jews," they laughed.

But Jesus hadn't done anything wrong, and He knew it. This was all a part of God's plan.

When the soldiers came, some of Jesus' disciples were afraid and ran away. Others, like Peter, hung around to hear what was happening. Peter was warming himself by a fire when a servant girl asked him, "Aren't you one of those guys who was with Jesus?"

"No," Peter said. "It wasn't me."

Another girl asked, "Are you sure? You look like him."

"It wasn't me!" Peter said.

More people came up. "We're sure you're that guy."

"I don't know Jesus," Peter lied. "I've never known Jesus."

Then the rooster crowed, *caw-ca-cah*, and Peter ran away and cried and cried.

Good Friday

from Matthew 27; Mark 15; Luke 23; John 19

People didn't understand. Jesus was God's perfect Son, sent to earth to save them from their sins. The leaders brought Him to the Roman governor, who put Jesus on trial. Many people were against Him. "Crucify Him!" the crowd shouted. "Kill Him! Nail His hands and feet to a big wooden cross!"

Jesus didn't deserve this. He had spent His time on earth loving and caring about people, helping them to know about His Father in heaven, and telling them the right way to live so they could one day join Him there.

Dying on a cross like a criminal was a sad but very important part of God's big plan. And Jesus would do it. He wasn't a criminal, but He would die like one.

The soldiers built a heavy wooden cross and nailed a sign to it that said: JESUS OF NAZARETH, THE KING OF THE JEWS. Then they marched Jesus through the streets. They made Him go up a hill to the place called the Skull. And then—they nailed Jesus to the cross. They also crucified two criminals with Him—one on His right and one on His left.

It was so painful, but still Jesus prayed, "Father, forgive these people. They don't understand."

"Why don't You save Yourself?" someone laughed. And of course, Jesus could have saved Himself—if He wanted to. A crew of angels would have rushed down from heaven to rescue Him if He had asked. But instead, Jesus chose to stay there on the cross and die to save all those who believe in Him.

No one could ever love as much as Jesus.

Then it happened: God poured all of His people's sin—in the past, now, and forever—into Jesus' heart. "Father!" Jesus cried. "Don't leave Me!" But God had to turn away from all the sin. And Jesus felt all the dirt of sin and all the anger of His Father that came with it. But it wasn't His sin. It was ours. Jesus felt it and suffered for it so that we wouldn't have to.

Right then, at that very minute, the world changed forever. Now God's people had hope. By asking God's forgiveness for their sins and believing in what Jesus had done for them, their hearts could be made clean, and they could live in God's perfect heaven forever.

At noon, an eerie, dark cloud filled the sky and hid the sun. Powerful lightning and thunder jerked across the sky. God's mighty anger at sin came down. The earth shook furiously. Huge rocks shattered and split. The sky swirled with dark, scary colors.

"Father, I give You My life," Jesus said. Then He looked up toward heaven and cried out, "It is finished!" and He died.

And it *was* finished. Jesus had done it! He had taken on Himself God the Father's anger and the punishment that was meant for His children, to save us from our sin.

Jesus Calling

*For God loved the world so much that he gave
his only Son, so that everyone who believes in him
may not die but have eternal life.*

JOHN 3:16 GNT

Yes, I died for you. But don't be sad.
Be happy that I love you so much.
I want you to be with Me, every minute, every day,
forever. If you ask Me to be your Savior,
we'll be together in heaven someday—
because I died for your sins.

Easter Sunday

from Matthew 27–28; Luke 24

God's big plan wasn't done yet. Some people still doubted that Jesus was God's Son. Even His friends weren't sure. You see, Jesus had told people that three days after He died, He would live again.

Jesus' friends laid his body in a tomb. The Roman soldiers came and sealed the tomb shut with a huge stone so no one could get in and take Jesus' body. Then they guarded the tomb night and day.

Those who hated Jesus figured He was dead and this was the end. Those who loved Jesus were almost afraid to hope.

Early Sunday morning, women who were friends of Jesus arrived at the tomb. Suddenly, the earth rumbled and shook. A blinding bright light tumbled down from heaven, and an angel appeared wearing a glowing white robe. He rolled the stone away from the tomb and sat on it. The sight of the angel and the empty tomb scared the guards so much that they fainted.

"Are you looking for Jesus?" the angel asked the women.

"He's not here. God brought Him to life, just as Jesus said He would. Hurry! Tell His disciples that Jesus has risen from the dead."

The women ran and told the disciples, but the disciples said, "Nonsense!" They sat around looking sad, refusing to believe that Jesus was alive.

Later that day, two of them were walking to a village called Emmaus when a stranger came and walked along with them. "What are you discussing?" He asked.

"What everyone else is talking about," one of the disciples answered. "Have you not been here the past three days?" Then they told the whole story of what had happened to Jesus.

After the stranger heard this, He said, "Why are you so slow to believe?" He reminded them of everything the prophets had written about Jesus, and especially the part where Jesus would come back to life.

When they got to Emmaus, the disciples invited the man to have supper with them. He sat at their table, took some bread, blessed it, and broke it. Then He passed it to them. That's when they realized: They knew Him!

"Lord Jesus!" they cried out. "It's You!" Then suddenly, Jesus disappeared.

They found the other disciples and told them what had happened. "He's alive!" they agreed. "Our Lord Jesus lives!"

Jesus Calling

[Jesus] is not here; he has risen!

LUKE 24:6

My Power is stronger than death. I rose from the dead—
I became alive again! If you believe in Me
and ask Me to come into your heart, heaven is
your future home. You will live with Me forever,
even when your life on earth is over.
This is the best gift anyone could ever give you!

Doubting Thomas | from John 20

Now Thomas had not yet seen Jesus, and he doubted. "I need to touch the nail holes in His hands," he said. "I need to see the place in His side where the soldier stuck Him with a spear before I will believe He is alive."

The disciples were meeting in a room with the door shut tight. Suddenly, Jesus showed up, right in the middle of them all. It was a miracle!

Jesus held out His hands and showed His scars. "Touch the places where the nails went in, Thomas. Feel the spot on My side where the spear pierced Me."

Finally, Thomas believed. "You are Jesus," he said, "my Lord and my God."

"Thomas, you have seen Me and believed. Blessed are those people who haven't seen Me and still believe anyway," Jesus said.

Jesus Goes to Heaven | from Luke 24; John 14

If you think your work for Me is over, then you are mistaken," Jesus told His disciples. "Your work is just beginning. You must go to all the people in all the countries of the world and tell them everything that has happened to Me. To be forgiven for their sins, they must repent and believe in Me and what I have done. If they do this, then their hearts will be turned toward God."

Jesus said this to His disciples, but He meant it for everyone who follows Him. God wants everyone who loves Jesus to tell their families and friends about Him. This was the next part of God's big plan so that Christ's church could grow in countries all over the world.

Finally the time came for Jesus to say goodbye, but just for a while. He was going back to heaven to prepare a place for everyone who believes, so that someday, when their bodies died and their souls went to heaven, their home would be ready for them to live in.

Jesus and His disciples went outside. He raised His hands and blessed them. And then, just as if He stood in an elevator, Jesus went up . . . up . . . up . . . into heaven.

Jesus Calling

"After I have done this, I will come back and take you with me. Then we will be together."

JOHN 14:3 CEV

I am always with you in spirit. You cannot see Me with your eyes, but I am always by your side. For now, you see Me only with spiritual eyes— the eyes of your heart. Someday, though, when your body dies, you will see Me in person. I will come back and take you with Me to heaven. We will be together forever!

Joy Came Down | from Acts 2

Jesus promised to always be with God's people, even after
He went back to heaven. But how could that be? Well, God had
a special surprise waiting—the Holy Spirit.

Some followers of Jesus were in an upstairs room of a house
when a mighty rushing wind came down from heaven. Bursts
of fire skipped in all directions and danced on the wind. Then,
what looked like tongues of fire settled on each person.
This was not typical fire—this was the promised Holy Spirit!

Joy filled their hearts like it never had before—it was a joyful love so powerful that they had to tell everyone. Jesus' Holy Spirit had come down from heaven. "Hallelujah!" the Christians shouted. "Praise God!"

On that very day, people from all over the world were in Jerusalem to celebrate Pentecost. When they heard the disciples loudly speaking their different languages, people were shocked and came running to see what was going on. "Aren't these uneducated men from Galilee? How can they speak all these many languages?"

But some people made fun of them. "Look at those crazy Jesus followers," they said. "What's wrong with them now?"

But nothing was wrong. Everything was so right. Jesus lived in their hearts.

Peter stood up. He shouted to the crowd, "Listen to my words. Everything you've heard about Jesus is true. If you don't believe me, read the Old Testament. Read what the prophets had to say. Jesus came to save us from sin. Evil men crucified Him on a cross, but God raised Him from the dead. He went up to heaven, and now He's sent us the Holy Spirit. This is why you see us so filled with joy. It's Jesus' love filling our hearts. He has come to live in our hearts forever!"

After the people heard this, some of them wanted Jesus in their hearts too. "What should we do to have Jesus live in our hearts?" they asked.

"Repent and be baptized," Peter said, "and you will be forgiven and receive the gift of the Holy Spirit." On that day, 3,000 people believed in Jesus as their Savior and were baptized.

"Hurray!" said the disciples. "Now let's go and tell the whole world about Jesus." And that's what they did. Just like Jesus had told them to do, they set out and told people about Jesus' amazing love. They started many churches this way.

Jesus Calling

"The Spirit will teach you everything and will remind you of what I said while I was with you."

JOHN 14:26 CEV

I have a special gift for everyone who believes in Me.
The Holy Spirit comes and lives inside you.
My Spirit fills you with Love, Joy, and Peace.
He is your Helper on good days and on bad days too.
The Spirit helps you know what is right and what
is wrong. He also helps you *do* what is right.

Philip and the Ethiopian | from Acts 8

After Jesus' disciples went their separate ways, an angel of the Lord told one of them, Philip, to head south on a road that led out of Jerusalem. He heard the sound of horses' hooves. *Clippity-clop, clippity-clop.* Then Philip saw a chariot with a very important-looking man inside. "Go up to that chariot," the Spirit said to Philip's heart.

The man was reading the Old Testament, the book of Isaiah. "Hello," Philip called, and the chariot stopped. "Do you understand what you're reading?"

"No," the man said. "Is the prophet talking about himself or someone else?" He was reading Isaiah's prophecies about Jesus— the Suffering Servant who would save people from God's punishment.

Philip offered to explain, and the man asked him to ride along.

"I am from Ethiopia, and I want to know about God," the man said.

So Philip told him all about Jesus and God's plan and how Jesus died for our sins. He explained that everyone who follows Jesus will never be separated from God and will live forever in heaven.

The Ethiopian wanted forever-life for himself. So when the two of them came to some water, the Ethiopian asked Jesus to come into his heart, and Philip baptized him. Then the Spirit of the Lord took Philip away to a different place to tell more people about Jesus, and the Ethiopian went home happy all the way.

Jesus Calling

By one Man's obedience many will be made righteous.

ROMANS 5:19 NKJV

Because I obeyed My Father by dying on the cross, people can be saved and live with Me forever. Because Philip was obedient, the Ethiopian was able to share the good news about Me with his family and other people in his country. When you obey Me and tell people about Me, you bless them with a wonderful gift. And you will be blessed too.

Saul | from Acts 9

I'm so smart and important, Saul thought as he traveled to Damascus. Saul was a well-known Jewish religious teacher, and he was very proud. He was also someone who was feared by those who followed Jesus.

On this trip, like so many times before, he was on his way to get rid of people who followed Jesus. But God had other plans . . .

Suddenly, a bright white light shot from heaven and blinded Saul. "I can't see!" Saul yelled as he stumbled to the ground.

"Saul, why do you hate Me?" said a deep, booming voice.

"Who are You, Lord?" Saul asked.

"I'm Jesus," the voice answered. "Go to the city of Damascus and wait for Me there."

Saul waited in Damascus, terribly afraid and unable to see. But Jesus did not leave him without help. He sent His friend Ananias to Saul. "Lay your hands on him," Jesus said. "I want Saul to see and be filled with My Holy Spirit." So Ananias put his hands on Saul's head. Something that looked like fish scales fell from Saul's eyes, and he could see again! All at once, Jesus' Spirit filled his heart with love and joy.

Saul, the one who hated Jesus, became one of Jesus' most famous followers—the disciple named Paul.

Jesus Calling

God did not send his Son into the world to condemn its people. He sent him to save them!

JOHN 3:17 CEV

I want to live in the hearts of people all around the world. I invite people to come to Me no matter what they've done in the past. What matters is today. If people—young or old—ask Me to forgive their sins, I will be their Best Friend forever. I want to be *your* Best Friend.

Peter and the Angel   from Acts 12

Arrest that man!"

A big guard grabbed Peter and threw him into a dark, dirty jail cell. People did not like that he was spreading the word about Jesus and His love. The whole church prayed for Peter, worried that he might be hurt—or worse.

Peter slept in a jail cell, chained to the wall with soldiers guarding him. But that didn't stop Jesus. "Peter, wake up!" He felt someone poke him in his side. He rubbed his eyes, wondering if he really saw an angel standing there in front of him.

"Follow me," the angel said. Just like that, the chains fell off Peter's hands. He followed the angel right out of the jail!

Amazed, Peter went to a house where some friends were praying. He knocked on the door, but when a young servant girl came to answer and heard his voice, she was so shocked that she left him outside! Finally, they let him in! Everyone was so happy. The angel had set Peter free to tell even more people about Jesus' love.

Jesus Calling

*[God's] miracles are marvelous,
more than we can count.*

JOB 5:9 CEV

Sometimes you may think you are in an impossible
situation. You may think there is no way out,
no answer to your problem. But remember:
With Me there is *always* a way, *always* an answer.
With Me, nothing is impossible! So ask for My help,
and trust Me to do what is best.

Lydia Believes | from Acts 16

God sent Paul on many faraway adventures. He traveled to foreign cities in Asia, sailed across the sea to Europe, and taught about Jesus in Greece. One day, Paul and his companions walked down by a river where a group of women sat praying. A woman named Lydia, who owned her own business and sold purple cloth, began to ask Paul questions.

"I worship God, but I feel like something is missing," she told Paul. "I'm a sinner, and I can't please God." She hadn't yet heard about Jesus and His plan.

When Paul told her that Jesus had taken the punishment for her sins, Lydia couldn't wait to accept Jesus and be baptized. "Now my heart is clean!" she said. Then Lydia opened her home to Paul and his friends.

Lydia finally understood that knowing God the Father isn't enough. She needed Jesus too.

Jesus Calling

"I am the way, the truth, and the life.
No one comes to the Father except through Me."

JOHN 14:6 NKJV

As hard as you try, you cannot get to heaven on your own. Everyone does some bad things—all boys and girls, even mommies, daddies, and teachers. And there is no place in heaven for sin. This is why you need Me in your heart. I am your only Way to heaven. I am the One who washes away your sins and opens the way to God the Father.

The Jailer and the Earthquake | from Acts 16

Peter wasn't the only one thrown into jail for talking about Jesus. Paul, too, was willing to do what God wanted . . . even when it was really dangerous!

"Get in there!" the jailer shouted as he threw Paul and his friend Silas into a cold, dirty cell and chained their feet to heavy blocks of wood. They couldn't escape, but that didn't stop them from sharing the good news.

What do you think they did in jail? They sang praises to God so the other prisoners could hear!

Around midnight, a terrible earthquake suddenly shook the jail. The thick walls wobbled; the strong doors opened; the chains fell off the prisoners. But Paul and Silas stayed put.

The jailer awoke and saw the open doors and broken chains. "Oh no!" he cried. He would be in serious trouble if the prisoners escaped.

"It's okay! We're all here," Paul and Silas answered. The jailer fell at their feet. Surely God was in this.

"Sirs, what should I do to be saved?" he asked.

"Believe in the Lord Jesus, and you will be saved," said Paul. "You and everyone in your household!" The jailer believed, and he set Paul and Silas free. That very night, they baptized the jailer and his whole family. More people had a forever home in heaven.

Jesus Calling

"If the Son sets you free, you will be free indeed."

JOHN 8:36

Even while Paul and Silas sat in chains in prison, they were still free. They had been set free from sin in their hearts. I can do the same thing for you. Come to Me and ask Me to forgive your sin so your heart will be free.

Paul and the Unknown God | from Acts 17

The city was bustling with people. "Outta my way!" someone shouted as he pushed through the busy street.

"How much for that chicken?" someone hollered in the marketplace.

"Oh, great and mighty block of stone," said a man as he worshiped a statue. *A statue?!*

When Paul found an altar in the main city in Greece with the words "To an Unknown God," he knew that the people who lived there really needed Jesus. "People of Athens," Paul shouted, "let me tell you about the real God! He isn't a statue. He lives in heaven. He made you, and the sky and the earth, and everything else.

"God loves you, and He sent His Son to take the punishment for the bad things we do. Jesus died, and God brought Him back to life. He's making a place in heaven for all who repent and believe."

When the people heard about God raising Jesus from the dead, some laughed. Others walked away. But a few believed in Jesus and worked with Paul to spread the good news and begin new churches for Jesus.

Jesus Calling

[Paul said to the people in Greece,] "It is in [God] that we live and move and keep on living. Some of your own men have written, 'We are God's children.'"

ACTS 17:28 NLV

You live *in Me*! Because you are My child, the most important thing about you is not what *you* do but what I've already done—died for your sins. You don't have to be really good at something to be special. Since you are Mine, you're *already* special!

Paul's Shipwreck | from Acts 27

Paul was arrested for telling so many people about Jesus. Soon he was put on a ship with other prisoners, headed for Rome, where he would have to stand before a judge in court.

"It's a bad time to sail," he warned the crew. "The winter winds are howling. We might have trouble." But who would listen to a prisoner?

Paul was right. A vicious storm came. Waves like mountains crashed into the ship, and the sailors fought hard to keep it afloat. "Help!" they cried.

Below deck, Paul whispered, "God, help us." Then an angel appeared with a message. Paul hurried to tell the crew. "Listen!" he shouted over the thunder and wind. "God promised me that I'll get to Rome. Anyone traveling with me will be safe. Have faith and believe."

Paul was sure that God would save them, even when the ship drifted near an island and—*CR-AACK!*—it broke into pieces. "Swim!" someone shouted. The crew and the prisoners all jumped overboard and swam safely to shore.

God still wasn't done with Paul. He had more work for him to do.

Jesus Calling

God is our safe place and our strength.
He is always our help when we are in trouble.

PSALM 46:1 NLV

Storms come to everyone. Sometimes they are bad-weather storms that destroy things and scare you. Sometimes storms are sad things that happen, and sometimes they are tough times. Do not worry about what storms may come your way. Just trust Me and hold on to My hand. I will be your Safe Place and your Strength.

Paul the Writer
Letters from God | from The Epistles of Paul

M y dear friends . . ."

Paul wrote many letters to Jesus' followers who were members
of new churches. God whispered the words to Paul, and he wrote
them down. Paul's letters reminded the followers to live the right way—
like God wanted them to. The letters taught them to love people,
to love the Truth, and to obey God.

God sent the Holy Spirit to fill Paul with words for the believers in many cities. God wanted Paul to encourage them when they were ready to give up. So Paul wrote letters that said, "Be joyful. Rejoice! Don't worry about anything. Have faith in God, and always hope."

Often God needed to correct wrong teaching among His people. Paul's letters helped the people keep their eyes on God, happily working for Him as members of the church.

Paul the Writer

The Fruit of the Spirit | from Galatians 5

In one of his letters, Paul wrote about the fruit of the Spirit—
how the Holy Spirit changes Christians as He works in their hearts.
When the Spirit lives inside, He makes His fruit—love, joy, peace,
patience, kindness, goodness, faithfulness, gentleness, and self-
control—grow in a person's life. This is the way Jesus lived,
and we should want to become more like Him.

The Armor of God | from Ephesians 6

Paul also wrote about weapons we can use against Satan. Since there were many Roman soldiers walking around back then, Paul spoke of the parts of a soldier's armor as a way to help Jesus' followers remember the weapons God gives us for fighting our enemy.

"Put on the belt of truth," Paul wrote, "and right living as your chest protector. Wear the good news of peace on your feet, and carry a shield of faith. Your helmet is Jesus' gift of salvation, and your sword is the Bible."

Paul knew that we need to be on guard against Satan's evil tricks and use the protection God gives us.

Jesus Calling

Your word is a lamp to my feet and a light for my path.

PSALM 119:105

My Word, the Bible, is a gift for you. Paul was one of the writers of the Bible. The Holy Spirit helped Paul and the others write God's truth without making mistakes. Read My Word, and think about what it means. You will learn more about Me and how much I love you. The Bible is a light for you—to help you "see" Me better.

249

Paul the Writer

Young Believers | from 1 Timothy 4

Paul's young friend Timothy was the pastor of a new church.
He did a lot of things right—helping others, encouraging their
faith. Yet sometimes Timothy was unsure of himself, and sometimes
he was afraid. What if people ignored him because of his age?

"Don't let anyone put you down because you are young,"
Paul wrote to his friend. "Set an example by the way you act.
Love people the way God loves them, and grow in your faith
in Jesus. Live a good life.

"Read your Bible every day, and always be ready to listen, help, and teach," Paul told Timothy. "If you do all these things, people will hear you and respect you no matter how old you are."

Timothy was a very young man, but he did what Paul said and learned from him. God can use anyone who is willing to listen and obey.

Timothy became a great church leader. His example is a good reminder that God can use young people as well as older people to serve Jesus.

Jesus Calling

You are young, but do not let anyone treat you as if you were not important. Be an example to show the believers how they should live. Show them with your words, with the way you live, with your love, with your faith, and with your pure life.

1 TIMOTHY 4:12 ICB

It doesn't matter how young or how old you are. I live in you, and I can do important things through you. I want you to be kind to others—brothers, sisters, parents, friends. You can show your love for Me by loving other people. You don't have to be big to do big things for Me!

John's Dream | from The Book of Revelation

When John the disciple was old, he was sent away to an island as punishment for talking about the Lord. Jesus appeared to him there, glowing and magnificent. He showed John the final part of God's plan. "Write it down," Jesus said, "so the whole world will know."

A peaceful silence wrapped around John. Then Jesus showed John what things would be like at the end of time.

Satan and all his followers, with their mean, dirty tricks, would be kicked off the earth forever. People who loved Jesus would live in God's perfect, shimmering city with golden streets and gleaming pearl gates—a heavenly city like no one had ever seen, on a brand-new earth. "See?" God said. "I am doing a wonderful new thing!"

Jesus promised that, one day, things will become perfect the way God wants them to be. Someday God's love—brighter than the brightest sun—will be the only light we need.

Finally, in the vision that Jesus showed to John, God and His children lived together as one perfect, happy family—the way it was supposed to be back in the Garden with Adam and Eve all those years ago.

Everything that John wrote down is real. He got to see into the future nearly 2,000 years ago, but one day all of this will really happen. When it does, Jesus will come back and take His followers to their forever home, just as God planned.

"I am the Beginning and the End," Jesus said. And John knew it was true: Jesus is coming back, and everything is going to be all right for those who believe in Him. No more sadness. No more tears. No sickness, darkness, storms, or fears.

"When?" John asked Jesus. "When will this wonderful part of God's plan happen?"

"That," said Jesus, "is still God's secret. But I'm coming. So be ready."

Sitting there on the island, John wrote the last words ever written about God's big plan. You'll find them at the end of the Bible:

Come, Lord Jesus. Come quickly, and His grace be with all His people. Amen.

Jesus Calling

"Pay close attention! Come to me and live."

ISAIAH 55:3 CEV

Come to Me, My child. Spend time getting to know Me better. Remember that I am with you always—all the time and everywhere you are. I have oceans of Love for you!

I want you to understand more and more of this wonderful Story about Me—because it's also a Story about *you*! This amazing adventure goes on and on and on—into your forever-home in heaven. This Story never ends because My Love for you never ends.